Never Out of the Hole

Tips and Tactics for Winning at Match-Play Golf

T. J. Tomasi, Ph.D.,
Mike Adams,
and Michael Corcoran

An Owl Book

Henry Holt and Company . New York

Henry Holt and Company, LLC
Publishers since 1866
115 West 18th Street
New York, New York 10011

Henry Holt® is a registered trademark
of Henry Holt and Company, LLC

Published in Canada by Fitzhenry & Whiteside Ltd.,
195 Allstate Parkway, Markham, Ontario L3R 4T8.

Library of Congress Cataloging-in-Publication Data
Tomasi, T. J., date.
Never out of the hole: tips and tactics for winning at
match-play golf / by T. J. Tomasi,
Mike Adams, and Michael Corcoran.—1st ed.
p.   cm.
"An Owl book."
Includes index.
ISBN 0-8050-5938-5 (pbk.: alk. paper)
1. Golf.   I. Adams, Mike   II. Corcoran, Mike.   III. Title.
GV965.A323   1999
796.352—dc21   99-17534
CIP

Henry Holt books are available for special promotions and premiums.
For details contact: Director, Special Markets.

First Edition 1999

Designed by Kate Nichols

Printed in the United States of America
All first editions are printed on acid-free paper. ∞

1 2 3 4 5 6 7 8 9 10

Contents

Introduction:
The Match-Play Tradition
in Golf

The title of this book, *Never Out of the Hole: Tips and Tactics for Winning at Match-Play Golf*, describes a mental state that is fundamental to winning at match play, the oldest form of competitive golf. In perhaps a more familiar voice, this sentiment is expressed in the classic line from legendary Green Bay Packer coach Vince Lombardi, who said, "Winning isn't everything, but wanting to win is." To be match-play tough—to carry yourself in a winning manner—means to believe earnestly that you can and will win every single hole no matter how grim the circumstances appear at any given time. All of the best match players in history have played with that single thought in mind, including the greatest match player of them all, Bobby Jones.

The Holy Grail of professional golf is what is known as the Grand Slam, an accomplishment that would require winning all of golf's four major championships in a single season. It has never been accomplished in the modern era of golf. Ben Hogan is the only player to come close, which he did in 1953 by winning the Masters, the U.S. Open, and the British Open.

Back before there was a Masters (which was first played in 1934), Jones did win the Grand Slam as an amateur. In fact, to win the Grand Slam in Jones's day, a player *had* to be an amateur, because the four major championships were made up of the U.S. Open, the U.S. Amateur, the British Open, and the British Amateur. A career amateur, Jones is really the patron saint of the everyday golfer. You see, all of the major amateur events that Jones won were played at match play, and match play is the format that everyday golfers have played since the game was first played. In 1930, Jones swept the big four, winning the British Amateur at the Old Course at St. Andrews, Scotland, and the U.S. Amateur at Merion Golf Club's East Course. He won those finals, in order, by scores of 7 and 6, and 8 and 7. (In match play, scores are recorded by the number of holes won as opposed to the number of strokes taken. For example, when Jones won the British Amateur final 7 and 6, that score means he was seven holes ahead with only six holes left to play, i.e., it was a mathematical impossibility for his opponent to win.)

Since this book is about how to win at match play, you may wonder why it begins with this brief look at Bobby Jones. The answer is that, in a day when long-hitting automatons rule the professional game, you and your weekend golfing buddies have more in common with Jones than you do with Tiger Woods or David Duval. As much as you would like to, you don't play the same game as those fellows do. For you, the game is a struggle against yourself, the course, *and* an opponent. The authors thought you might take a little comfort in knowing that the game was also a struggle for the only player who ever won the Grand Slam.

Jones's international competitive career began in 1916 when he was just fourteen years old. That year he entered the U.S. Amateur at Merion, and in his first round match he drew Eben Byers, who was a former U.S. Amateur champion. Years later, the great amateur Chick Evans recalled "scanning the golf course and seeing Bobby and Eben Byers engaged in a club-throwing competition.

People took this as a sign that he [Jones] would be a failure." Without question, it was an auspicious and obnoxious debut for the future champion. But while some shook their heads, Evans saw the matter differently. "Here was a golfer of tender years," said Evans, "whose heart was really broken by a poor shot." This was the fiercely competitive side of Jones, who managed to make it through to the quarterfinals that year, at an age that would today make him a freshman in high school. (Not even Tiger Woods can top that!) Jones reached the finals in the next U.S. Amateur in 1919 at Oakmont (the 1917 and 1918 editions were canceled due to World War I), before losing in the finals 5 and 4.

In 1921, Jones went to Scotland for the first time to play in the Amateur and Open of Great Britain. The British Open was held at the Old Course, and Jones found himself in contention after two rounds. In the third round, however, he was unable to cope with the quirks of that fabled course, the wind, and himself. (Sound familiar?) He shot 46 on the front nine and started the inward half with a double-bogey six followed by five shots to reach the green at the par-three eleventh hole. He then picked up his ball, shredded his scorecard, and stomped into the clubhouse. His antics were viewed as outrageous.

That summer he entered the U.S. Amateur at St. Louis Country Club and made it to the quarterfinals where he met Willie Hunter, the reigning British Amateur champion. Hunter was one up through thirty-five holes (it was a thirty-six-hole match), when Jones skulled his approach shot over the green and, in a spasm of immaturity, wildly flung his club after the ball. The club struck a woman spectator in the leg. Fittingly, Jones lost the match.

When Jones returned home to Atlanta, he found a letter waiting for him from George Walker, president of the United States Golf Association (USGA), the governing body of golf in the United States and the organization that conducts the national championships. The letter ended, "You will never play in a USGA event again unless you learn to control your temper."

After reading that letter, Jones never again threw a club in competition.

In 1923, Jones won the first of his total of thirteen major championships by taking the U.S. Open at Inwood. He won the thirteen titles in just eight years, and from 1924 to 1928, Jones had the following finishes in the U.S. Amateur: first, first, second, first, first. This book contains segments called "Masters of Match Play." Jones is not included among them because he is talked about here. Each of the "Masters of Match Play" segments ends with a little bit of instruction you can learn from the great players. From Bobby Jones you can learn the greatest lesson of all: Defeat your own demons first, and you can beat anyone at the game of golf.

In match play, much of the pressure is self-applied. This book will teach you how to overcome that *and* to apply pressure on your opponent. There are things in this book that seemingly go against Jones's reputation as the nicest guy who ever played the game. They are presented with the assumption that you aren't going to use them in the finals of the U.S. Amateur, but rather in an attempt to take a few harmless bucks off your buddies on Saturday afternoon. We don't recommend using any of the gamesmanship ploys in your club championship because you should conduct yourself with integrity during such competitions. But when it comes to the five-dollar Nassau with automatic two-down presses, anything goes, partner. Jones, a man who liked to have a whiskey now and again, would probably give you a wink and say, "Let's get it on, mister."

form of play for the masses: A single slipup in stroke play can eliminate a player from contention in the event because he must carry that mistake along with him to the end of the competition. In other words, a screwup on Thursday still counts on Saturday. Match play is more forgiving. Make a small goof in match play, and the bad news is over the moment that hole is over. It provides the breathing room everyday golfers need to compete at something that is not a full-time pursuit. For all the accolades professional golfers receive, the fact remains that they are full-time golfers. It is realistic for them to be expected to produce superb stroke-play scores, much the same way a superb chef is expected to produce a meal that is extraordinary in comparison to your mother-in-law's pot roast. Since the everyday player plays mostly for fun and relaxation, match play has a built-in margin of error that prevents a round from becoming an exercise in futility.

The establishment of match play as the primary type of competition in golf dates back to a time well before golf was a common game in the United States, and involves some of golf's most legendary characters, such as Willie Park, Old Tom Morris, and his son, Young Tom. The Morrises, father and son, and Park were each multiple winners of the British Open in the early days of that event, which was the first of the modern major championships. First played in 1860, the Open was the only regular stroke-play event in Great Britain, and involved only a handful of players. Since the Open was played only once a year and the players wanted to compete more frequently, the big guns of the day focused their talents on money matches, played for the most part at courses in Scotland. These matches were major events when they occurred—whole towns would turn out to watch the Morrises take on Willie Park and his chosen partner. The betting was frantic among the watchers, and the competitors vied for a pot put up by local rich guys. In an 1855 one-on-one match between Old Tom and Park, the frenzied crowd practically rioted when Old Tom quit the match because Park supporters interfered with his ball.

Never Out of the Hole

I.

The Nature of
Match Play

Match play has long been the most common method of determining the winner in a test of golfing skills. This is true despite the fact that most professional events are contested at cumulative stroke play over four rounds. Professional golf, for all of its carnival appeal and high drama, is a blip on the map of golf—the total rounds played in professional events each year are a microfraction of those played by Joe Golfer at private clubs, resorts, and municipal courses across the country. Here is how *The Rules of Golf* defines match play: "In match play the game is played by holes. Except as otherwise provided in the Rules, a hole is won by the side which holes its ball in fewer strokes. In a handicap match, the lower net score wins the hole. The reckoning of holes is kept by the terms: so many 'holes up' or 'all square,' and so many 'to play.' A side is dormie when it is as many holes up as there are holes remaining to be played." *The Rules* goes on to tell us that "a match is won by the side which is leading by a number of holes greater than the number of holes remaining to be played."

There is a simple reason why match play remains the primary

Never Out of the Hole

I.

The Nature of
Match Play

Match play has long been the most common method of determining the winner in a test of golfing skills. This is true despite the fact that most professional events are contested at cumulative stroke play over four rounds. Professional golf, for all of its carnival appeal and high drama, is a blip on the map of golf—the total rounds played in professional events each year are a microfraction of those played by Joe Golfer at private clubs, resorts, and municipal courses across the country. Here is how *The Rules of Golf* defines match play: "In match play the game is played by holes. Except as otherwise provided in the Rules, a hole is won by the side which holes its ball in fewer strokes. In a handicap match, the lower net score wins the hole. The reckoning of holes is kept by the terms: so many 'holes up' or 'all square,' and so many 'to play.' A side is dormie when it is as many holes up as there are holes remaining to be played." *The Rules* goes on to tell us that "a match is won by the side which is leading by a number of holes greater than the number of holes remaining to be played."

There is a simple reason why match play remains the primary

form of play for the masses: A single slipup in stroke play can eliminate a player from contention in the event because he must carry that mistake along with him to the end of the competition. In other words, a screwup on Thursday still counts on Saturday. Match play is more forgiving. Make a small goof in match play, and the bad news is over the moment that hole is over. It provides the breathing room everyday golfers need to compete at something that is not a full-time pursuit. For all the accolades professional golfers receive, the fact remains that they are full-time golfers. It is realistic for them to be expected to produce superb stroke-play scores, much the same way a superb chef is expected to produce a meal that is extraordinary in comparison to your mother-in-law's pot roast. Since the everyday player plays mostly for fun and relaxation, match play has a built-in margin of error that prevents a round from becoming an exercise in futility.

The establishment of match play as the primary type of competition in golf dates back to a time well before golf was a common game in the United States, and involves some of golf's most legendary characters, such as Willie Park, Old Tom Morris, and his son, Young Tom. The Morrises, father and son, and Park were each multiple winners of the British Open in the early days of that event, which was the first of the modern major championships. First played in 1860, the Open was the only regular stroke-play event in Great Britain, and involved only a handful of players. Since the Open was played only once a year and the players wanted to compete more frequently, the big guns of the day focused their talents on money matches, played for the most part at courses in Scotland. These matches were major events when they occurred—whole towns would turn out to watch the Morrises take on Willie Park and his chosen partner. The betting was frantic among the watchers, and the competitors vied for a pot put up by local rich guys. In an 1855 one-on-one match between Old Tom and Park, the frenzied crowd practically rioted when Old Tom quit the match because Park supporters interfered with his ball.

THE RYDER CUP:
MATCH PLAY AT ITS BEST

This book contains many references to the Ryder Cup and the records of certain individuals in that event. The Ryder Cup has evolved into golf's single most exciting event and it is conducted purely at match play. What is it that is so appealing to fans about the Ryder Cup? First, it is one of the few times we get to see the world's best players go at it at match play. Second, it provides great theater, allowing golf fans a glimpse of what it would be like if golf were an Olympic event. The pressure created by playing for one's country makes the Ryder Cup a crucible for today's stars, and requires them to show their true competitive grit to anyone who cares to watch. There is little question that the players with the best Ryder Cup records—especially those from 1983 to the present—are the best match players in the world.

The reason 1983 is used as a point of delineation is that it marked the first close match in what has become a biannual brawl without peer in professional golf. To fully understand the measure of the event, it is necessary to digress for a moment. The Ryder Cup was first played in 1927 and, save for the years during World War II when there was no competition, has been played on a regular basis every other year. Up until 1973, the United States team took on an opponent made up of players solely from Great Britain, and had won the matches sixteen times with only two losses and one tie. In 1973, players from the Republic of Ireland were added to the British side in an attempt to help balance the lopsided affairs, but it didn't help much—the United States continued to rout the Great Britain and Ireland team. Things began to shift in 1979, however, when any player from the European Tour's Order of Merit (that tour's money list) was permitted to play as long as he was born in Great Britain, Ireland, or continental Europe. From that point on, the matches were never the same. It took a few years to build up some steam, but once the European squad got its bearings the matches became a donnybrook. The 1983 Cup didn't give any hint of being different—the United States had won handily in 1979 and 1981 despite the combined strength of Team

Europe. But in 1983, playing on its home turf at PGA National in Florida, the United States squad was pushed to the limit, and only last-day singles matches heroics by Lanny Wadkins and Tom Watson staved off a European victory. (Within the context of a larger team competition, a "singles match" occurs when one player competes directly against another player, neither player having a partner.) In 1985, in England at The Belfry, the European team hammered the Americans, and the Ryder Cup as we now know it took full flight. In 1987 the Europeans did what up until that time had been considered inconceivable—they beat the Americans on United States soil at Muirfield Village. Not only did they beat the Americans, they beat an American team captained by none other than Jack Nicklaus, and on a course he had built! Since then, it has been impossible to predict who will win each meeting, and the only certainty is that it will come down to a desperate few holes with the world's most talented players trying to avoid choking under the extreme pressure.

The appeal of the Ryder Cup to the average fan is even greater when you consider that it offers multiple formats within the three days of play. Each of the first two days of play offers foursomes (one ball played at alternate turns by partners) and four-balls (the best ball of partners being the lone score that counts on a given hole). While you may not play much in the way of alternate-shot competition, you certainly play your fair share of best-ball contests. So there is a familiarity to the proceedings every other September when the Cup is played. In all likelihood, you have no clue what it's like to play in a seventy-two-hole stroke-play event, but if you've played in a member-guest tournament, you know what it's like to play team match play stretched over several days. Similarly, you've probably played many head-to-head eighteen-hole solo matches in your day, and that's the same format used on the final day of the Ryder Cup. One of the main reasons cited for golf's popularity among hundreds of millions of people worldwide is that the pros play the same game as the wannabes. But it is only at the Ryder Cup that we see the top players truly playing the same games as the everyday golfers—and suffering the same nerves we all feel when faced with a par putt to win a five-dollar Nassau.

(A Nassau is a three-point money match, with one point available for the most holes won on the front side, another point available for the most holes won on the back side, and the final point available for the most holes won overall. In a five-dollar Nassau, each point is worth five dollars.)

Finally, the changing face of the Ryder Cup has had another huge impact on the game from the fans' perspective. The boost in confidence European players received from realizing they could play with and beat the Americans led them to become a bigger factor in the major championships each season. Since the European team became competitive in 1983, we have seen Bernhard Langer of Germany win two Masters, Nick Faldo of England win three Masters and three British Opens, Ian Woosnam of Wales win the Masters, Sandy Lyle of Scotland win a Masters and a British Open, and Jose Maria Olazabal win a Masters. Seve Ballesteros, who had already won two Masters and one British Open before the 1983 Ryder Cup, went on to win two more British Opens.

(It's kind of comical to imagine that scene, and to then recall the closing holes of the 1997 U.S. Open at Congressional when the crowd was obviously pulling against Scotsman Colin Montgomerie *and* for South African Ernie Els and American Tom Lehman. When Montgomerie prepared to play a crucial putt at the penultimate hole and visibly reacted to the sentiment against him, the crowd hooted and hissed at him. In his post-round interview, he acted as if he'd been the victim of a crime against humanity!) In fact, for a short period of time, betting on matches was banned in St. Andrews because there were too many people fighting duels—actual pistol duels!—over the outcome.

As much fun as it is to look back at the Morris versus Park matches, you don't have to stretch your imagination much at all to see the direct connection between those matches and the majority of matches in which you play. That link, of course, is money. Those matches of yesteryear wouldn't have interested many folks if there hadn't been some serious cabbage on the line, and nowadays most matches involve a little betting action in order to keep things interesting. Over the course of a golfer's life, most matches are simple money games. There are, of course, a few events a year you play for pride—club championships, better-ball team competitions, etc.— but either way you want to win. It's only human to want to win, even the most friendly of matches. As Ben Hogan once said, "I play with friends, but we don't play friendly games."

Regardless of whether you're playing to win the club championship, the St. Tropez Four-ball, or twenty dollars from Vinny and Caveman (the same two guys you've played every weekend for the past fifteen years), the goal of the game is the same: Win more holes than the other guy(s).

MASTERS OF MATCH PLAY: SEVE BALLESTEROS

In 1978, the British PGA sought the advice of Jack Nicklaus regarding how the Ryder Cup might be made more competitive. At the time, the Cup had lost nearly all of its luster, having evolved into a biannual rout of Great Britain and Ireland by the Americans. Nicklaus recommended widening the selection procedures, a suggestion that eventually led to the inclusion of players from outside the British Isles as long as they were from continental Europe. The most significant result of this action was that it paved the way for the entrance of Seve Ballesteros into the competition, forever changing the Ryder Cup.

Starting in 1979, Ballesteros played in every Ryder Cup save one (1981) until 1995. During his terrific tournament career, Ballesteros won five major titles and many championships, but it was in the Ryder Cup where he left his indelible mark on the game. His 20-12-5 Cup record earned 22½ points for the European team over the years, but it was Ballesteros's attitude and will to win that were his major contribution. More specifically, Ballesteros was able to transfer his massive energy and confidence to his usually more reserved British teammates. The result was a European team that played with passion and expected to win. He was able to impart this spirit to teammates even as a noncompetitor, when he captained Europe to victory in the 1997 Ryder Cup. (That Cup, incidentally, was played at Valderrama in Spain—a site selection that was truly a tip of the cap to Ballesteros for what he has meant to the event.)

There is much to be learned from the way Ballesteros approached match play. He was the perfect example of how you can hit some bad shots and still win a match. He exemplifies the proper competitive mind-set. He *always* felt that he was going to win—losing was never a consideration. And when Ballesteros did lose, he didn't let it deter him from feeling that he would certainly win his next match. It is interesting to note that in his ten losses between 1979 and 1993, eight of them occurred when he played with a partner and only two were solo. (Another interesting note is to *whom* Ballesteros lost: Lanny Wadkins was his opponent four times in a team match.)

What you can learn from Seve Ballesteros

In addition to being a fierce competitor, Seve was an excellent tactician. One technique he popularized was using the toe end of the clubface to strike the ball on fast, breaking downhill putts. For the most part, it was always considered fundamentally sound to strike all putts with the center of the clubface, i.e., the sweet spot. This presented a problem on very fast, breaking downhill putts, however, because the center spot on the putter-face is designed to produce maximum velocity with minimal effort, resulting in that they were hit too firmly and did not react to the slope of the ground, or putts that started off-line and never had a chance of going in. The reason for the latter type was that in an attempt to take something "off" the speed, a player would typically eliminate the follow-through portion of the stroke. This meant slowing the clubhead down as it approached the ball, a mistake that almost always led to the clubface opening and pushing the ball to the right of the intended line. Either way, players of all levels had trouble dealing with downhill breakers.

The tactical breakthrough perfected by Ballesteros accomplished two things: First, a ball played off the toe end of the clubface rolls very slowly. This deadening effect is magnified the farther toward the toe (and farther *from* the shaft and sweet spot) the ball is played. Second, using this technique allows you to follow through without imparting too much speed on the ball. The end result is a very slow-moving putt that starts on-line and reacts to the break in the manner necessary for the putt to be holed. If you try it, remember that it is intended for use only with a very short stroke— no more than an inch long going back and an inch through the ball.

How Match Play Differs from Stroke Play

Match play and stroke play are two separate species of the same game. Here's a list of the main ways in which the two forms of play differ:

- In stroke play (also referred to as medal play), you are playing against the entire field entered in the event and you must post a score for each hole. In match play, you need only concern yourself with one opponent at a time, and if you're out of a hole you can just pick the ball up, put it in your pocket, and move on to the next tee. (This is legal in match play.) The only thing you've lost is that hole.

- Since every stroke counts toward your bottom line in stroke play, the strategies are different than they are in match play, i.e., risks taken and not properly executed are more harmful in stroke play, which often leads to a more conservative strategy. An excellent example of this occurred at the 1998 Bay Hill Invitational, when John Daly attempted to carry a water hazard to reach the par-five sixth hole in two shots. His second shot came up just short. So he tried it again. And again. And again until he ended up with an 18 on the hole. Amazingly, Daly birdied the very next hole. If he'd been playing match play, his aggressive strategy would have been a good one—he'd have probably been level for the two holes at worst. As it was in stroke play, he was

12 over par for the two holes and out—way out—of the competition.

- In medal play, the size of the field means that you may be playing under different conditions than the rest of the field. You and your fellow competitors (the guys you play with, but not your partners) might play in the morning, when the grass is wet and the greens are soft, and another player might tee off six hours later, when the greens are firmer and maybe faster or slower, depending on the type of day and the type of grass. Or maybe it's windier in the later part of the day (it usually is until just before sunset). In match play, your opponent doesn't get any breaks regarding the conditions of play—you both play the same holes at the same time. This means you don't get any breaks, either.

- In match play, you can *see* what your opponent is doing and you know exactly what you need to win. In stroke play, you don't always know what you need to win, which has cost players big championships. (Sam Snead in the 1939 U.S. Open and Jesper Parnevik in the 1994 British Open are two examples. Both players pressed to make closing birdies when they didn't need them, the imagined pressure resulting in dramatic misfires.)

- In match play, there tends to be a certain amount of what is referred to as "gamesmanship," particularly between longtime rivals. Gamesmanship is not cheating, rather it's more like a mental wrestling match that goes along with the actual matching of shots. Some players look at gamesmanship as simply getting an edge. Others don't look so kindly on it. Whatever your view on it, gamesmanship is rare in stroke play.

- Match play is *very* personal. You're trying to beat some*one* (your opponent) not some*thing* (the golf course, the scoreboard). And no matter how noncompetitive you think you are, it just galls you to lose to another person. Match play takes on a very definite edge, since at the completion of the match there is little doubt about who the better player was on that day.

- In match play it's very common to have a partner. Typically speaking, this doesn't occur in stroke play. Which type of strategy you use on a given shot when playing with a partner depends in large part on the format of play. The two basic formats for partners are four-ball (better-ball partners) and foursomes (alternate shot). Four-ball is what is normally referred to as "better ball." You and your partner each play your own ball, and the better of the two counts for the team score on the hole (versus the best ball of your opponents). In foursomes, each team plays one ball, and the teammates play tee shots on every other hole—one plays the tee ball on all odd-numbered holes, and one plays the tee shot on all even-numbered holes. Once the ball is in play, the two alternate shots until the ball is holed. The easiest way to remember the difference between foursomes and four-ball is that there are four balls in play at the same time in a four-ball.

- If you watch a lot of pro-Tour events on television, you'll hear players mutter the same two boring things over and over: "The player who hits the most fairways and greens will win," and "The player with the hottest putter will win this week." Yawn. Match play is much more exciting and unpredictable. One of the great match players of all time is Seve Ballesteros, and over the course of his entire career he's hit fewer fairways than there are hairs on Sam Snead's head. As for putting, this may sound a bit unusual, but match play doesn't necessarily favor the better putter. In stroke play, you have to make every putt because you're playing against the entire field—you miss two or three four-footers and you're down the road. In match play, there are times when you simply don't have to putt. If your opponent is obviously going to lose the hole, he'll concede the hole to you. (A player can concede victory to his opponent on a given hole or the entire match at any point in the match.) This means if you just roll it up there pretty close, you're going to get a few given to you. There aren't any "gimmes" in medal play.

How each of these differences between stroke play and match play affects you depends on what type of player you are and what type of personality you have. The next chapter will help you identify your style of play and your opponent's style of play. These are the first two steps in becoming a superb match player.

GREAT MOMENTS IN THE RYDER CUP: 1969, ROYAL BIRKDALE, U.S. 16, GREAT BRITAIN 16— SHOULD YOU CONCEDE LIKE JACK DID?

When the American team captained by Sam Snead pulled into Royal Birkdale, they were heavy favorites. The team was loaded with talent, including Jack Nicklaus, Raymond Floyd, Lee Trevino, and Billy Casper, and faced a team made up mostly of the same guys they'd been trouncing for years, with one exception, Tony Jacklin. Earlier that year, Jacklin won the British Open, making him the only player on the Great Britain team that had won a major championship. A total of six matches were used in the format that year, and Jacklin stepped up to the tee in all six for the Brits. He won a total of five points, winning four of his matches and halving two. (In Ryder Cup play, a player or partnership wins a full point for a match won outright, and a half point for a match that ends in a tie. A match ending in a tie is called a *halve*.) It is one of those halves that has gone down in history.

The last day of competition that year featured two rounds of singles matches. In the morning set, Jacklin had throttled Nicklaus 4 and 3, setting up an afternoon rematch. As they stood on the eighteenth tee of their afternoon match they were all square (tied), and the matches overall were tied—15½ for the United States and 15½ for Great Britain. If either Nicklaus or Jacklin could win the hole outright, he'd win the Cup for his side. Both players faced par putts, with Nicklaus having the longer of the two. Upon holing his four-footer, Nicklaus promptly proceeded to concede the two-plus feet Jacklin had remaining, thus conceding a halve for the hole, his match, and the overall Ryder Cup. History unanimously regards Nicklaus's concession as a great act of sportsmanship, though legend has it (perhaps apocryphally) that Captain Snead gave Nicklaus an earful about giving away a chance for victory.

The question is, if you were faced with a similar situation in a match, what would you do? The answer, without fail, is to make your opponent putt. Never concede a putt to win a hole (unless you've picked up), and never concede a putt to win or halve any match or portion of your match (e.g., if you're playing a Nassau). Trust us—your humanitarian gestures aren't going to mean much when you're digging in your wallet for a twenty-dollar bill to pay Frankie Threeputt. Make your grand gestures in other areas of your life—and make Frankie putt whenever you think he might miss.

THE PGA CHAMPIONSHIP AT MATCH PLAY

From its first playing in 1916 until 1957, the PGA Championship was the only one of the modern major championships conducted at match play. The early years were a brutal test of match play, with every round of the competition made up of thirty-six holes. The first two rounds were medal-play qualifying (the lowest scores qualified for the match-play portion of the event), and from the second round play consisted of thirty-six-hole matches. This was the format from 1916 through 1934, with the exception of 1922, when qualifying and the first two rounds of match play were only eighteen holes. From 1934 through 1957, the format varied—some years there was no thirty-six-hole play until the quarterfinals, while other years it was thirty-six holes from qualifying straight on through to the finals.

While it was conducted at match play, the PGA Championship produced a diverse list of champions, which proved that at match play just about anything was possible. Some of the matches were almost unfathomable. In 1938, for instance, Paul Runyan won his second PGA Championship when he defeated Sam Snead in the finals. The fact that Runyan won is not so amazing—he was a great player—but it was the manner in which he did so. He crushed Snead 8 and 7 in what has become one of golf's classic David versus Goliath tales. Runyan was not a long hitter and Snead was the longest of his, or just about any other, era. Runyan was a short-game wizard and his style of play likely drove Snead crazy.

Snead's match in the semifinals that year was also a fine example of how match play differs from stroke play. In that match, Snead made four consecutive threes to finish the match one-up on Jimmy Hines. (To win one-up means a player had a one-hole advantage after completion of the final hole.) Had the two men been playing stroke play, Hines, at 8 under par on the day, would have defeated Snead by a stroke.

The match-play years helped to define some of the game's legends: Walter Hagen won five championships; Gene Sarazen, who would eventually become the first player to win each of the modern Majors at least once, won back-to-back in 1922–23, defeating Hagen in a thirty-eight-hole final in 1923. In fact, back-to-back winners were common in the early years—much more so than stroke-play events. "Long" Jim Barnes won the first two PGA Championships (1916 and 1919, interrupted by World War I), Sarazen's two were followed by four in a row by Hagen, which were followed by two in a row by Leo Diegel. Denny Shute pulled a double in 1936–37. Clearly, some players are more comfortable playing at match play. It doesn't mean they aren't good medal players (remember, they had to shoot low qualifying scores to get into the match-play portion of the event), but rather that the best stroke players aren't necessarily the best match players. Sarazen and Hagen were particularly brilliant. Sarazen qualified for match play in twenty-eight PGA Championships, played eighty-two matches, and won fifty-seven of them. He was the last man standing three times, his third coming in 1933 when he beat Willie Goggin in the finals.

The 1957 final marked the end of match play in the PGA Championship. Lionel Hebert beat Dow Finsterwald 2 and 1 to close out a part of the game's history that will most likely never be revived at the level of individual play. The reason for match play's demise? It made for bad television; since only a handful of matches were played when the championship was on the line, if one was a blowout it was boring to watch.

2.

The Nature of the Match Player

In the format known as match play, the key word is *match*. In fact, by adding another word to it, you can begin to clearly see the basis for your strategic thinking in match: "match up" play. Almost every sport uses the idea of match ups—in football a quarterback will consider how his receivers compare in terms of size and speed to the opposing defensive backs. If one of his receivers is taller than the defensive back that covers a certain side of the field, the quarterback may elect to throw the ball high and let his taller receiver go up and get it. This has to be balanced against the fact that the defensive back may have outstanding leaping ability, or is perhaps an excellent coverage man and can quickly judge the quarterback's intentions. It's a cat-and-mouse game, each of the participants poking and prodding the other to find weaknesses he can exploit with his own strengths.

In other sports, teams and opponents readying to face one another often have the luxury of viewing game films before they meet in battle. In golf, even if you did have film of an opponent, it wouldn't be too helpful because you can't tell much just by watching someone swing, and the conditions of play are always different.

Despite the drawbacks of not knowing much about your opponent, it is possible to familiarize yourself quickly with him and set your strategy. Doing so requires you to assess two people: yourself and your opponent. Since you should know your own game very well, the only possible pitfall you face in that area is a lack of honesty regarding your own potential and limitations. Assessing your opponent is a different matter. You must quickly come to some conclusions about him *and* how his game suits the venue for your match.

Getting a Line on Your Opponent

If you're observant, you might know the tendencies of your regular opponents. Notice we said *might,* because it's not unusual for someone to play matches against an individual for years and never really pay close attention to his strengths and weaknesses. So whether you've played against someone every weekend for the past nine years, or you're meeting him for the first time, the first step toward winning your match is to decide the makeup of your opponent. Since you need to determine this on the spot, we're going to show you how. No matter who you're playing, he will fall into one of the following three categories. As you read, try to determine which category you fit into, because it will come in handy later when we try to help you combat your own weaknesses.

1. **The Bomber.** The Bomber knows only one way to play, and that is to put the pedal to the metal. He'll use his driver on almost every hole, and feels that his length off the tee is his greatest asset. He is certain that he can intimidate others with his power, so he seldom backs off from displaying it. The Bomber is capable of great stretches of low scoring, and is equally capable of taking an X

on any given hole. Typically speaking, he will fire right at the flag no matter how dangerous it is to do so. Sometimes this pays off, and sometimes he gets burned. His two great weaknesses are inconsistency in ball flight and the fact that he is susceptible to his own temper—he hates it when a short, straight hitter starts to get the better of him, and typically can't handle it.

The Bomber's greatest strength contributes to one of his weaknesses, the dispersion factor. Since he generates tremendous clubhead speed the ball explodes from the club with great velocity. When the clubface is in any position other than square at impact, the ball is not going to fly on a straight line. The amount it misses that straight line is magnified by the speed at which the club is moving. The faster the club is moving, the more off-line a shot is going to be. This is the case especially with the driver, because the less loft a club has, the more sidespin it imparts on the ball. Sidespin is what makes the ball curve off-line. In other words, when the Bomber is making his biggest swing, he is using the club he is most likely to hit off-target—and into trouble. This contributes to the high scores he will almost certainly make on a few holes in your match.

These velocity-based errors also hurt him on his approach shots, even though these are played with more lofted clubs. He misses a lot of greens by a wide margin, often putting himself in places from which he can't get the ball close to the hole (or even on the green). To put this into perspective, a top-level PGA Tour participant hits about twelve greens in regulation per round. That means he misses six of them, so he's got to get up and down at least four times to be a few strokes under par (this assumes he makes a few birdies along the way). The Bombers you face are probably going to hit far fewer greens per round than a PGA Tour player. Their agenda is focused solely on distance. They are more concerned with outdriving you than with shooting the lowest score.

THE QUINTESSENTIAL BOMBER: John Daly.

YOUR BASIC STRATEGY AGAINST THE BOMBER: Be ready to

pounce when he misfires. Since you'll be hitting most of your approaches first, concentrate on getting the ball anywhere on the green (rather than attempting to hit it close to the hole) to apply some heat. He's emotional, he'll feel it.

2. **The Magician.** This is golf's version of Fred Sanford, the junk man. Good players often say of Magicians, "He can get up and down from a garbage can." As an opponent, the Magician is very tough on your psyche—you see him spray a wild tee shot and then you don't see him again until you reach the green. He is score oriented, and form doesn't mean a thing to him. If he has to play his approach shot off a cart path to beat you, he'll do it—or at least give it a try thinking he *can* do it. He will often attempt shots that seem perilous, because he has a magnificent short game and relies on it to bail him out of trouble. The downside to the Magician's game is that it's like a house of cards—if he's having a mediocre day with this short game, the house collapses. The Magician is an inconsistent ball striker on the majority of the holes he plays, but it doesn't phase him. Don't judge him on his ball striking.

The Magician relies so heavily on his brilliant short game that it doesn't take very much to throw him off. Take away just one percent of his short game and he is in big trouble, because his ball striking isn't good enough to carry him. (Nineteen ninety-six U.S. Open Champion Corey Pavin is a prime example.) The Magician's short game must be great in order for him to win—good isn't good enough. But be warned, the Magician is intrepid. He really never formulates a plan of attack for the entire round, so he *expects* to be in bad spots and expects to recover from them. You must always expect that he may hole any shot—the longest putt, the most difficult chip. Even on a bad day, it only takes one sensational shot to get him fired up again. The plus side to this is that he has high expectations of his short game, and when he doesn't meet them it is emotionally damaging to him. His brand of game could be called "manic" golf.

THE QUINTESSENTIAL MAGICIAN: Seve Ballesteros.

YOUR BASIC STRATEGY AGAINST THE MAGICIAN: As with the Bomber, you can kill the Magician with consistency, but it's tougher to accomplish. Your key is to stay focused because, like the Bomber, the Magician's mind tends to wander. You don't have to look for the openings—he'll provide them for you. Be prepared for a long match, though, because no lead is safe against the Magician.

3. **The Machine.** In the mind of the Machine, the entire round is a progression of shots from point to point. He sets a very precise plan of attack based on the course he's playing, and knows before he steps on the first tee where he wants to hit his tee shot on every hole. He also knows where he wants to hit his approach shots. He is focused on his own game and does not really care what you do as his opponent. He figures he has a better plan and believes that in the end that's all that matters. He depends on hitting fairways, hitting greens, and two-putting. He survives on your mistakes, but he doesn't care when you make them. In fact, he's not even paying attention to you. Machines have the stroke-play mentality of playing the course imbedded in their soul, and they can't change that, not even in match play. He is very swing oriented—he is much more concerned with form than with playing for the lowest score. His weakness, like that of everyone else, lies in his strength. If his plan goes awry—if things don't go systematically as he prefers—he's in trouble.

The Machine typically does not respond well to adversity. He is extremely uncomfortable when the situation forces him to deviate from his plan. The Machine is particularly vulnerable if you jump on him early, because he's counting on a long match and is waiting for you to screw up. He's not going to throw a lot of low numbers at you, but he's going to beat you on every hole where you screw up. If he hasn't caught you deep into the match, you can expect him to begin to unravel. A single poor shot on his part is typically the prelude to more poor shots. He probably thinks a little too much about form under the match-play gun.

THE QUINTESSENTIAL MACHINE: Pick any of the following who have won only U.S. Opens among the majors: Scott Simpson, Andy North, Curtis Strange, Hale Irwin. They are solid players, but seldom described as spectacular.

YOUR BASIC STRATEGY AGAINST THE MACHINE: If you can get an early lead and hold your game together through the late middle of the round, he'll start to press. By and large, he doesn't react well to this. If you can't seem to get ahead of him, you've got to start playing with his head. This is easier to do than you might realize, and will be covered a bit later in the book.

Hybrid Players

The Bomber, the Magician, and the Machine represent the three basic types of opponents you'll face in match play. At the level at which you probably play, almost every golfer will fit comfortably into one of these three categories. There are two hybrid variations on these three basic types, however. You aren't going to run into them every day, but when you do you will have your hands full, because these hybrids are the most difficult match-play opponents to beat.

1. **The Bomber/Magician.** In the above text, Seve Ballesteros is listed as the quintessential Magician. In reality, Ballesteros in his prime was a Bomber/Magician. Another example would be the very young Ben Crenshaw. As you can probably imagine, this hybrid type of player hits the ball a long way and combines that ability with a great knack for getting up and down when he misses a green. For the most part, these players have a great natural feel and rhythm for the game. They also combine the emotional elements of the Bomber and the Magician, relying more on being emotionally "up" than a pure Bomber or pure Magician. They are super-

emotional and either get swept up by the moment and play fantastically well, or get devoured by the moment and fall to pieces.

2. **The Machine/Magician.** The true Machine doesn't handle misfiring very well when he misses a green, because missing greens is not in his plan. The Machine/Magician, who may be the best match player of all, is capable of temporarily stepping outside his plan to deal with the situation at hand. The best example of this hybrid is Tom Kite, who took a very methodical approach to the game, but had a terrific short game that could get him back on track after a miscue. True to the Machine form, the Machine/Magician is not naturally blessed with a great short game, but rather works very hard to develop one. Kite practiced all elements of his game with a regularity uncommon even among PGA Tour players. This hybrid type is very tough mentally, and is truly vulnerable only against the Bomber/Magician when the latter is having his very best day, because no matter how hard the Machine/Magician tries, he is still rattled by his opponent's unexpected miracle shots.

A hybrid Bomber/Machine doesn't really exist. Perhaps the only one ever was Jack Nicklaus, but as with almost everything else in golf, Nicklaus is the exception that proves the rule. Big Jack was no magician but he didn't need to be—he had a Bomber's length and he was incredibly accurate. He had the Machine's sense of planning, and he seldom slipped off his predetermined track. He didn't have the uncanny chipping and pitching abilities of the Magician, but he was a lethal putter. And since he didn't miss many greens to begin with, it didn't matter much that he possessed only ordinary skills in the other half of his short game.

Golfer, Know Thyself

Part of the purpose of becoming familiar with the different types of match players is so that you can define which type you are. Other savvy match players will identify what type of player you are and forge *their* game plan against you based on this. It is help-ful to know what the other guy is counting on you to do—what he perceives as your weakness and the moments when he will attack.

In the best possible world, you'd like to be a hybrid player, but that isn't a practical goal for the average player due to the time constraints imposed by real life. If you're lucky enough to have the time to practice a lot, you should certainly strive to develop a hybrid game. If like most everyone you don't have the time, you're stuck with your basic type. This doesn't mean you can't win more often than you lose; it simply means you have to work with what you've got.

As you move through this book, you'll pick up a variety of ways to use your strengths. You must always keep in mind, how-ever, that you have to play *your* game. If you're a Bomber your best chance of winning is to play like a Bomber—don't back off just because you're up against a Machine. Likewise, if you're a planner, make your plan and stick to it and expect to execute it like a Machine. When you back off from your instinctive style of play you place yourself in unfamiliar territory and greatly reduce your chances of success. You see this frequently in stroke-play events, when a golfer builds a big lead by playing a certain way and then decides to change course in order to protect his lead. This tactic usually leads to that player's game falling apart just when he needs it most. Stay true to your overall game, but try to remain flexible. If you need to make a temporary adjustment to bail yourself out of a jam, do it. Then get right back to your nor-mal game on the next tee.

No matter how good a job you do at sticking to your game, you are going to get in some sticky situations in match play. Here's how to prepare for them and get out of them.

MASTERS OF MATCH PLAY:
LANNY WADKINS

If ever there was a John Wayne of golf, it was Lanny Wadkins. A longtime PGA Tour star and the 1977 PGA Championship winner, Wadkins justifiably earned his reputation as the most feared gunslinger in match-play golf. Wadkins was a killer at match play from early in his career. In 1970 he won the Southern Amateur and Western Amateur at match play. It was his second Southern Amateur, the first coming in 1968 at the age of nineteen. Wadkins also won the U.S. Amateur in 1970, during an unfortunate eight-year stretch when that event was contested at stroke play. He made his first appearance in the Ryder Cup in 1977 (at the time, the PGA Champion during a Cup year was automatically on the team) and went 3-0 that year, the only undefeated American on a team that included Jack Nicklaus, Tom Watson, and Ray Floyd. In 1983, with the Cup in the balance, Wadkins stiffed his wedge approach at the final hole to make a birdie and halve his match with Jose Maria Canizares of Spain. Tom Watson's victory over Bernard Gallacher gave the United States a one-point win. By the time Wadkins had finished his career as a Ryder Cup competitor, he had a record of 20-11-3, with a winning record in each of the three types of matches (4-2-2 in singles, 9-6-0 in foursomes, and 7-3-1 in four-balls) and had racked up a total of 21 points.

Similar to many great match players, Wadkins was supremely confident and aggressive on the course. The go-for-it nature of his game cost him more than a few stroke-play events, but it was perfectly suited to the challenges presented by match play. No matter how far Wadkins was from the hole, he fired directly at the flagstick. No shot was too demanding. (The fine teacher Jim McLean once said about Wadkins, "If the hole was a Frisbee floating in the middle of the ocean, Lanny would fire right at it and expect to hit it.") Like Ballesteros, Wadkins had limitless imagination on the course, which is a major ingredient in making the never-out-of-the-hole attitude a reality.

What you can learn from Lanny Wadkins

Wadkins was always a player who did things his own way. That's not at all unusual in greats, but what made Wadkins different was that his way violated conventional wisdom in golf. He didn't spend a lot of time on his preshot routine. His swing was a wild blur. He got mad when he hit a bad shot. He let his emotions rule him. He would rather go down in flames than lose for lack of trying—for lack of heart. The lesson to be learned from Wadkins is that there is logic to his approach, and it can work for you.

Wadkins did things quickly—from making decisions to swinging the club—because that was his nature. If you naturally do things quickly in everyday life—walking, talking, and assessing situations—you should apply this same manner to your game, regardless of what conventional golf wisdom dictates. Even if you've read a million times that you should swing slow, if it feels more natural to you to swing fast you should do so. Just be sure to keep the same tempo (pace of swing)—start fast and stay fast— and you can be fundamentally sound *and* have it feel good.

Another characteristic of Wadkins's game was that he didn't analyze shots to death, which is one of the things that made him a superb match player. If you are inclined to be a go-for-broke player, you should consider only the most basic facts regarding the shot you face—working out every last detail will only supply you with reasons *not* to go for it. Start thinking that way and you won't be playing *your* game. The basic facts to consider: How far is it to clear *X*? Can you carry the ball that far with your typical shot? Can you carry it that far with your best shot? If you have a personality like that of Wadkins, the answers to those three questions should provide you with enough information for any shot you face, depending on the situation. If you know the yardage and can answer the second question yes, you fire right at the flag. If you answer the second question no, but the third question yes, you quickly consider what type of player you're up against and how your match stands. If you decide to go for it, expect to execute your plan and make a confident swing—just like Lanny would.

The Bomber in Trouble: Improve upon
Your Weaknesses

If you're a Bomber, the most common error you're going to make is missing the green either left or right, because the velocity of your shots is going to cause you to spray them sometimes. And when you do miss the green left or right, you're going to miss it by a lot. In other words, you're going to be pitching the ball, not chipping it. Typically when you miss to the sides of the green, you're going to encounter two things: lousy lies and bunkers that you need to carry. One of the biggest steps you can take to counter these troubles is to carry a sixty-degree L-wedge in your bag.

Learning to play the L-wedge effectively requires patience, but it will pay off. First of all, in your setup, you should get most of your weight on your left side (about a 65/35 split) and keep it there throughout the swing. The swing with the L-wedge is tricky and differs from most other short-game shots. If you make an arms-only swing with the L-wedge, the club will go right underneath the ball, barely moving it. So the second step is to make a mini body turn both away from and through the ball. To start the swing, turn your left hip back a little at the same time that your arms swing back. When you swing the club through the ball, turn your right hip through the ball as well. The third point for effectively using the L-wedge is to maintain constant clubhead speed throughout the shot—don't slow down through impact. It takes a lot of practice, but you have to train your brain to realize you can swing hard and hit a twenty-yard shot.

One final note on playing the L-wedge: You should go through your usual preshot routine, because when you get misaligned with the L-wedge, you're probably going to undercut the ball or catch it thin. Start by picking out a target, which is the spot where you want to land the ball on the green or the collar of the green. Then pick an intermediate target between your ball and your actual target. Make it something just a few inches ahead of the ball, like a twig or an off-color blade of grass. Next, set the lead edge of the clubhead square to your intermediate target. Then step into position to play the shot, placing your feet, hips, and shoulders on a line parallel to your target line. There is no need to open up the face of the club or your body position—the extreme loft of the club will do the work for you.

The quality of the recovery shot you play is dictated in large part by the lie of the ball. This is important, because frequently you're upset or rattled after having played a poor approach, and you're not interested in playing these dinky shots. It's imperative that you focus on what type of shot the lie gives you. If the back of the ball is clear and you can get at it cleanly with the clubface, you can play a standard pitch shot as described above. If the back of the ball is obscured or covered over by grass, you'll want to play a "sand" shot by making a long, lazy swing and using the grass underneath the ball as a cushion. The third type of lie is a perched lie, where the ball is actually sitting on top of the grass. For this type of lie, you'll want to hover the club over the ball at address—don't ground it. Play the ball toward the middle of your stance and pick it off the grass by placing the clubface directly on the back of the ball.

Aside from missing greens on the wide sides, you face another unique challenge as a Bomber: You'll tend to get a lot of buried lies in bunkers because your approaches will enter the sand at a very steep angle. (Because you hit the ball hard, it flies higher and descends at a sharper angle.) This is especially the case when you're hitting your approach shots into the wind, which will make your ball fly higher than normal. The first way of dealing with this is to temper your aggressiveness on approach shots into the wind. This doesn't mean you shouldn't fire at the flag like you always do, it just means you should play a different shot. For example, if you are at what is normally nine-iron distance for you, recognize the fact that the nine-iron is going to fly very high into the wind. Instead of the nine-iron, take a seven-iron and choke down almost to the steel on the grip, then make your normal swing. This two-club drop will produce a lower ball flight that will hold the line better into the wind.

When a miscue occurs and you do end up with a buried lie in the sand, you should know how to deal with it. First, select your pitching wedge to play the shot. The pitching wedge doesn't have any bounce, and on this type of shot you want the club to dig into the sand rather than deflect off it as it would if you used your sand wedge. Next, lean toward the target. (Another way of thinking of this is to lean your spine ahead of the ball.) Once you're set, make a very upright backswing (all arms) and slam the club into the sand directly behind the ball. There is no follow-through. Expect the ball to pop out onto the green and run quite a bit. You won't have much control over it, but at least you'll be out of the sand.

The Magician in Trouble: Practice
Your Strengths

If you're a Magician you have to practice the way you play. Since you're intrepid, you don't have much of a plan when you play, and your practice should reflect that. Your ability to stay in a match depends entirely upon your short game. When you hit the ball all over the lot you never know what type of lie you're going to end up with, so your practice routine is simple. Stand in the middle of a practice green with a bag of practice balls and randomly throw them twenty to thirty yards around the green. Scatter them all over the place. Then take your wedges and play the balls as you find them—don't touch or adjust the lie. This will help you to be prepared for anything that might happen out on the course.

The Machine in Trouble: Monitor
Your Rounds

You're methodical, working your way around the course with a plan you set before the match begins. The best approach for you to keep your game together is to monitor each round for errors to determine what you're going to do in your next practice session.

After each round, sit down and mentally replay the round, taking note of the errors you made. Your errors are typically pretty glaring, because when your ball flight goes screwy it's very noticeable. The next time you practice, devote the first part of your session to working on your most recent weakness. Once you feel you have it covered, spend the remainder of your practice time working on your strengths, which in your case are the fundamentals and swing mechanics. Once you have your errors corrected, consider them gone for the moment. Don't look at them as permanent weaknesses. Simply address your weaknesses as they appear.

The other key for you is to recognize that the time to fix your mechanical problems is not during a match. If you lose your swing in the middle of a match, try to notice if you're misfiring in a predictable pattern. If you are, try to allow for it. If it's unpredictable, play more conservatively, holding back on attempting shots you're uncertain about. Either way, don't try to fix your swing out on the course. Focusing on your swing instead of the shots you're playing is one of the guaranteed ways of taking yourself entirely out of a match.

The Common Traits of Great Match Players: Winning Is an Attitude

Whether they are Bombers, Magicians, or Machines, the very best match players share certain mental characteristics. Winning is an attitude, and nowhere is that more true than in match-play golf, where physical capabilities count for less than state of mind. You have to be a dogged competitor in match play. Someone once said that most people quit just before something good is going to happen, and it's surprising how often that is the case. For example, Jimmy Valvano and North Carolina State won the NCAA basketball championship in 1983. Before the final game, Valvano kept saying his team didn't have much of a chance. All he wanted, he said, was for his kids to hang in there until the last three minutes of

GREAT MOMENTS IN THE RYDER CUP:
WATSON AND NICKLAUS—BEFORE THE SPANISH
ARMADA, THEY RULED THE WAVES

For all of their dominance in the world of golf between 1975 and 1985, Tom Watson and Jack Nicklaus amazingly appeared only twice as teammates in the Ryder Cup. In 1977, on the first day of the competition, the two played a foursomes match (alternate shot) versus Tommy Horton and Mark James. The Americans won the match on the fourteenth hole.

In 1981, Captain Dave Marr had a good idea. He paired Watson and Nicklaus together for two solid days. In the first morning's match, Watson and Nicklaus took on Nick Faldo and Peter Oosterhuis and beat them 4 and 3. The next morning they met Spain's Jose Maria Canizares and Ireland's Des Smyth, and beat them 3 and 2. Since the two best players of their era were just hitting stride, Marr sent Nicklaus and Watson out again in the afternoon against Manuel Pinero and Bernhard Langer. Jack and Tom dusted them 3 and 2.

Those four victories in four attempts made Watson and Nicklaus the second most successful American pairing in Ryder Cup history. For the record, Arnold Palmer and Gardner Dickinson were 5-0 as partners.

"Jack had all the qualities you could want in a Ryder Cup partner," said Watson. "He was a gutsy team player. If I made a mistake, I knew he could make up for it. If he made a mistake, everyone knew he could recover. He definitely brought an intimidation factor. As a twosome, our whole was worth more than the sum of its parts, like Ballesteros and Olazabal became for Europe."

the game. He felt his team could beat anyone in those last three minutes, and they did just that. Even if you remember that game and say, "Hey, they had to make a last-second shot to do it," the point is that they were in position to win. They waited for something good to happen and they were in position to take advantage. Maybe it's not going to happen in every match you play, but if you aren't in position when it does happen, you're going to lose more often than not. Even if you lose the first four holes, you've got to stay with it because in all likelihood your opponent is eventually going to make a couple of mistakes. Once you quit mentally you're in big trouble, and it's almost a cinch that you won't be capable of pulling yourself together when your opponent hits a rocky patch of play.

Here's a list of the mental characteristics of great match players.

- **They feel like winners.** The best match players are convinced they are going to win before the match starts and at every point during the match. Even if they're losing, they can conjure up ways to win. If they do lose, they never carry it with them to the next match.
- **They never question themselves.** A great match player never questions whether or not he can win or pull off a shot. As soon as you start to question yourself, you're history. A great example of this was the last day of the Ryder Cup in 1991. In the singles matches, Mark Calcavecchia had a four-hole lead with four holes to play in his match against Colin Montgomerie. With the match seemingly sewn up, Calcavecchia managed to choke in a manner that is almost unparalleled in Cup history—he lost every one of the final four holes to halve the match. If Bernhard Langer hadn't missed a six-foot par putt on the final hole of his match with Hale Irwin (the last match of the day), Calcavecchia's collapse (the biggest since the fall of Rome) would have cost the United States the Ryder Cup.
- **They don't surprise easily.** In the 1977 British Open, Tom Watson and Jack Nicklaus battled it out over the last two days in what essentially was a match-play contest. Watson shot 65–65 versus Nicklaus's 65–66. On the eighteenth hole of the final round, Nicklaus had a thirty-two-foot putt

for birdie while Watson's ball was sitting close to the hole for birdie as well. As Nicklaus stalked his putt, Watson's caddie Alfie Fyles sidled up next to his man and said, "I suspect he'll get this one close." Watson shot back, "I expect him to make it." And Nicklaus did make it! But it didn't rattle Watson because he'd been expecting it.

- **They thrive on competition.** In the motion picture *Apocalypse Now,* the character played by Robert Duvall stands on the beach in the early morning and says, "I love the smell of napalm in the morning." Sick? Absolutely. Would you want him on your side in a fight? Absolutely. The deadliest match players love the notion of going head-to-head against someone—they want the fight, they want to mix it up. The more pressure the situation involves, the better they play.

- **They are unsentimental in combat.** Take a look at the Ryder Cup records of individual players in this chapter. One of the worst records of any American is Ben Crenshaw at 3-8-1. When you consider that this is a player who has won two Masters titles, that record is pathetic. Why? Crenshaw is a man who gets swept up in the moment in the worst possible way for a competitor—he is so aware of the historical significance of what is going on around him that he's unable to focus on his game. In plain speak, he's soft. This is different than the explosive emotion of someone like Seve Ballesteros, who lets his emotions gush forth *after* he's accomplished something. A golfer like Crenshaw is overtaken by his emotions before he gets to the first tee.

- **They act like they've been there before.** Unlike the NFL, where players react to every decent play they make as if they'd just single-handedly conquered Rome, great match players have a presence about them that lets their opponent (and anyone watching) know they are good. If they birdie the first hole to win, they don't punch the air defiantly—

they simply move on to the next tee. They do show their emotions when the match takes a dramatic swing, but this typically occurs toward the end of a match.

- **They are alert.** All good match players know where the match stands at all times, and they notice the tendencies of their opponents. As 1956 Masters Champion Jack Burke, Jr., once said, "Everything with its head down gets eaten—pigs, cows, sheep—they all get eaten. Lions, they don't get eaten, because they're always alert." You should watch your opponent like a hawk, but don't stare at him. It's best if you pay attention to what he's doing without making it too obvious. You want to try and guess when your opponent's performance is about to change during a match, and the only way you can do that is by watching every move he makes. The other part of being alert is to make mental notes on the positions of the flagsticks as you make your way around the course. Any time you pass by a green that you haven't played yet, check the position of the flag so you don't have to guess when you play the hole later on.

- **They never quit.** The same can be said of all great competitors, but it still should be pointed out. Until they are mathematically eliminated from a match, the best match players feel they can come back. In the above example with Montgomerie and Calcavecchia, things would have been much different if Montgomerie had thrown in the towel when he was four down with four to play. But he didn't.

There's no question that golf is an emotional game and some people react and play better when they get mad. John McEnroe, during the height of his tennis career, was a perfect example of that attitude. In golf, guys like Curtis Strange, Craig Stadler, and Lanny Wadkins all had pretty good tempers. Among the current big names, Tom Lehman can get pretty steamed out there.

HOW GOOD ARE THEY?

Since professional golfers are (for better or worse) the standard by which all golfers measure themselves, we thought it would be fun for you to look at the following Ryder Cup records to see how the big names have fared in match play.

U.S. Players

Player	Ryder Cup Record	Type of Player
Paul Azinger	5-7-2	Magician
Chip Beck	6-2-1	Machine
Julius Boros	9-3-4	Machine
Jack Burke, Jr.	7-1-0	Machine/Magician
Mark Calcavecchia	5-5-1	Bomber
Billy Casper	20-10-7	Machine/Magician
Fred Couples	7-9-4	Bomber/Magician
Ben Crenshaw	3-8-1	Bomber/Magician
Gardner Dickinson	9-1-0	Machine
Raymond Floyd	12-16-3	Magician
Al Geiberger	5-1-3	Machine
Hubert Green	4-3-0	Magician
Walter Hagen	7-1-1	Magician
Scott Hoch	2-0-1	Machine
Ben Hogan	3-0-0	Machine
Hale Irwin	13-5-2	Machine
Peter Jacobsen	2-4-0	Magician
Lee Janzen	2-3-0	Machine
Tom Kite	15-9-4	Machine/Magician
Tom Lehman	3-2-2	Bomber
Justin Leonard	0-2-2	Machine/Magician
Gene Littler	14-5-8	Machine
Davis Love III	5-8-0	Bomber
Mark McCumber	2-1-0	Bomber
Johnny Miller	2-2-2	Bomber
Larry Mize	1-1-2	Magician
Byron Nelson	3-1-0	Machine
Jack Nicklaus	17-8-3	Bomber/Machine

Player	Ryder Cup Record	Type of Player
Andy North	0-3-0	Machine
Mark O'Meara	4-7-1	Machine/Magician
Arnold Palmer	22-8-2	Bomber
Corey Pavin	8-5-0	Magician
Calvin Peete	4-2-1	Machine
Paul Runyan	2-2-0	Machine/Magician
Gene Sarazen	7-2-3	Bomber
Sam Snead	10-2-1	Bomber
Craig Stadler	4-2-2	Bomber/Magician
Payne Stewart	8-7-1	Bomber
Dave Stockton	3-1-1	Machine/Magician
Curtis Strange	6-9-2	Machine
Lee Trevino	17-7-6	Magician
Ken Venturi	1-3-0	Machine
Lanny Wadkins	20-11-3	Bomber/Magician
Tom Watson	10-4-1	Bomber/Magician
Tom Weiskopf	7-2-1	Bomber
Tiger Woods	1-3-1	Bomber/Magician
Fuzzy Zoeller	1-8-1	Bomber

European Players

Seve Ballesteros	20-12-5	Bomber/Magician
Brian Barnes	10-14-1	Bomber
Ken Brown	4-9-0	Machine
Howard Clark	7-7-1	Bomber
Eamonn Darcy	1-8-2	Bomber
Nick Faldo	23-19-4	Machine
Tony Jacklin	13-14-6	Machine
Mark James	8-15-1	Machine
Bernhard Langer	18-15-5	Machine
Sandy Lyle	7-9-2	Bomber
Colin Montgomerie	9-6-3	Machine
Jose Maria Olazabal	14-8-3	Machine/Magician
Constantino Rocca	6-5-0	Bomber
Sam Torrance	7-15-6	Bomber
Ian Woosnam	14-12-5	Bomber

Of course, there are other people whose games go to hell when they get mad. Paul Runyan was famous for getting opponents so irritated that they couldn't play. He always said he had an advantage because he was small, and bigger guys *hate* losing to little guys even though golf has nothing to do with how big you are. And Runyan had a cocky attitude to begin with, so that just pissed everyone off even more.

Your individual state of mind and temper play different roles in match play than in stroke play. In stroke play, the standard advice is to do everything you can to keep your temper under control, especially since the mistakes in stroke play add up over the course of several days. In match play, we suggest that you let your natural disposition drive you. If you're an excitable guy and you get mad from time to time, then go ahead and let out when you need to, and then move on. Don't try to be Mary Poppins if you're the Texas Chainsaw Murderer. Trying to suppress your nature will just turn your personality into a weakness. Get mad and get over it—don't let it poison the rest of your round.

The idea of playing in a state of grace with an inner calm is nice if you're playing in the All-Saints Match-Play Championship (and you happen to be Saint Francis of Assisi), but by and large that matches up with few personalities. Ky Laffoon, a Tour player back in the 1930s, was a perfect example of this. He once missed a putt and punched himself so hard that he dropped to his knees on the green. If he putted poorly during a tournament, he would hang his putter out the door of his car and drag it along the road as he drove to the next tournament site. But Ky Laffoon could play—he was the first Tour competitor ever to average under seventy strokes per round for a full season. He was a volcano—but once he let it out, he was a heck of a player.

3.

The Art of the Match

The first two chapters should have helped you to understand what match play is and the basic nature of competitors during a match. However, every match you play in will take a different route to its completion. Understanding the nuances of what is transpiring during your match *as they happen* is basic to your success in a specific match. This is true no matter how much you know about your opponent, or how much you *think* you know about your opponent, because no golfer (including you) ever really knows what kind of game he's got on a given day until the bullets start flying.

Breaking Down the Match

Not all competitive matches are eighteen holes, but for the purposes of analyzing the art of the match, we'll assume the match is one regulation round. (Some championships have thirty-six-hole matches, even at the club level. There are also gambling matches that break an eighteen-hole round down into three or more "mini" matches within one larger match. Gambling matches are covered in a later chapter.)

As you stand on the first tee of a match, it helps to break it down into three phases, which we'll call the *sparring* phase, the *setup* phase, and the *finishing-off* phase. Each phase consists of six holes, and each has a very specific goal. In the sparring phase your goal is to gather information about your opponent without losing any significant ground to him. In the setup phase you're going to start to build your lead, and in the finishing-off phase you're going to close out your opponent. (The final phase is covered in the next chapter, "Going for the Kill.") Keep in mind that not every match you play is going to follow this pattern, and that those that do won't always follow it in the strictest sense. The three-phase approach is intended to be a rough outline for you to follow during a typical match.

During the sparring phase of a match (holes one through six), you should be focusing mainly on two things: keeping mistakes to a minimum and observing the strengths and weaknesses of your opponent. To accomplish the first goal of avoiding an early deficit, you should be focusing on a couple of thoughts. First, even if you're a Bomber, you want to get the first few tee shots in play. Consider hitting a three-wood or another fairway wood. As has been noted time and again, matches last a long time, so even if you're a power player, you're going to have time to exploit that strength. Be patient. Hitting a few fairways to get the round started will help you gain confidence to swing away at the ball as you enter the second phase of the match. Just because you're sparring in the early holes doesn't mean you want to give holes away with wild tee shots. Give yourself a chance to get into the rhythm of the match and get comfortable with your swing for the day.

Second, be sure not to get sloppy around the greens during the early phase of the match. As the match wears on, you might have to start getting aggressive with your putter and short game, which means you're inevitably going to have some knee-knockers on the green. In these early stages of the match, however, you want to be certain you don't leave yourself any nerve-rattling putts that, if missed, could snowball into a bad day of putting. Try not to leave yourself any short ones above the hole. In other words, if you leave your approach shot to the green below the hole, make certain you don't charge the ball five feet past the hole on your first putt. The same logic holds if you are above the hole with your approach—don't leave your approach putt or chip short, placing you in a spot where you face a downhill tester on the first few holes. The reason for this is that you can make a more solid, confident stroke on a short uphill putt, and the ball won't break as much. In short, uphill putts are easier to make.

You should also be watching your opponent closely in between your own shots. Remember, this isn't stroke play. You can't ignore what your opponent is doing even if you're a Machine. That stuff about playing the course and not your opponent is only going to take you so far, so it's best to learn as much as you can about him early so you can concentrate on your own game as the match heads down the stretch. What sorts of things should you be looking for? First, you'll want to try to classify your opponent. Is he a Bomber, a Magician, a Machine, or a hybrid player? Knowing this will help shape your strategy as you move on. Next, watch him intently on the greens. Does he look nervous if he leaves himself a short putt, especially if it's a tough one? If he does, you should consider conceding a few of those types of putts early on in the match when you have a putt to win the hole. (In other words, if he's counting on your missing and his making his putt for a halve.) This is a smart move if you've played your cards right and left yourself an uphill putt (or a very short putt of any type) you feel confident you can make. The logic behind this is that you have a chance to win the hole and you are denying him the chance to build any feel or confidence with difficult short putts. If you miss, you still haven't lost any ground and he still hasn't had the chance to get in a groove with his putter. (You might be

GREAT MOMENTS IN THE RYDER CUP:
1995, TOM LEHMAN VERSUS SEVE BALLESTEROS

In the 1995 Ryder Cup at Oak Hill, Seve Ballesteros was playing Tom Lehman in the Sunday singles matches. The match was viewed as a pivotal one, since Ballesteros was the emotional leader of the European team. Lehman was also one of the American team's anchors that year, and when it came to battling the Spanish icon, Lehman was no shrinking violet. On the tenth hole, Lehman had a fairly long putt and he rolled the ball up near enough to the hole that he expected Ballesteros to concede the remainder to him. Ballesteros was away after Lehman's putt, and in broken English he said something that Lehman interpreted as a concession of the putt. Lehman picked up his ball and Ballesteros confronted him saying he had *not* conceded the putt and that he had actually requested that Lehman mark the ball. Perceiving this as one of Seve's legendary attempts at gamesmanship, the fans started hooting and hollering and booing, and a Rules official was called in. After some discussion, it was decided that Lehman should replace his ball and mark it. It turned out that Seve simply wanted to use the mark as an indicator on the line for his own putt. Whether it was gamesmanship or not is open to debate, but it was perfectly legal and Lehman recognized that fact. In fact, after the matter had been resolved, Lehman even held up his hands to ask the fans to stop booing. In the end, the incident may have only served to fire up Lehman. He went on to soundly defeat Ballesteros.

thinking that if you miss one or two of these putts, it might hurt your confidence. But even if you halve the hole you haven't *lost* anything and you are building an advantage for a hole soon to follow. Besides, you are playing with confidence, like all great match players do. Right?) One final note on this point: Never concede a putt that will win the hole for your opponent unless it is literally a tap-in of six inches or less.

If you're a Magician, you want to make certain you apply the same "leave-it-below-the-hole" logic the first few times you have to chip or pitch. (Hopefully, if you're a Bomber, you'll have played some smart tee shots and managed to hit the first few greens.) Now is not the time to try to hole out chips and pitches. Focus on giving yourself "good leaves" (to borrow from pool-hall parlance) that you can confidently ram home.

Of course, there's always a chance you might run into a buzz saw on the first few holes and have someone throw a few birdies at you. Don't panic. Unless you're playing a guy having a career day, he'll fall into his normal game after a few holes. Fast starts are common, but they don't last all day (that's why they call them fast *starts*). Most golfers are incapable of sustaining abnormally fine play over a full round.

In addition to watching your opponent's game, you should be sorting out how you feel in the early going. Does the club feel good in your hands? Are you thinking clearly before each shot? Are you remembering to go through your preshot routine, focusing especially on your target selection and alignment? Before the match moves into its second phase, you should have a good handle on what you feel you're capable of that day.

The Setup Phase

The second set of six holes in your match is the setup phase—the point in the match where you set your man up and position yourself for a strong finish. This is the part of the match where you should start to out-think your opponent and take advantage of every mistake he makes. (This isn't to suggest you shouldn't take advantage of mistakes in the sparring phase of your match, but you really should concentrate on getting your own game on track in the early going.)

Taking Advantage When Your Opponent Is in Trouble

When your opponent hits a tee shot out of bounds or into the trees, or he hits a shot that ends up in the water, you feel as if you should capitalize on his mistake and win the hole. For the most part, this is correct. If your opponent is obviously in trouble, you should adjust your strategy for the hole, but it doesn't necessarily mean you can assume you're going to win the hole. You adjust your strategy to ensure the worst you can do is halve the hole and increase your odds of winning the hole.

When your opponent is in trouble, your main goal becomes getting the ball on the green in the fewest number of shots involving the fewest number of risks. For example, if you face a 220-yard carry over water, that's a pretty big risk, so you don't want to go for it. The first thing you should do to reduce the risk factor is to make sure you don't aim any shot so that if you hit it straight you'll end up in trouble. If your opponent is in the boondocks and you are the biggest slicer in the world and you're facing a tee shot with trouble on the left, do not aim at the trouble assuming the ball is going to slice back. Such an assumption might result in your being in trouble, too.

The second important element of reducing your risks is playing smart layup shots. If you are going to play safe, then *play safe*. How many times has the following happened to you: Your opponent is in the bushes somewhere and you decide you're going to lay up short of the hazard near the green. You figure you have 180 yards to the edge of the hazard and you normally hit your five-iron 180 yards, so you take your six-iron and make a nice, smooth swing at the ball. And because you make such a nice, smooth swing, the ball flies perfectly from the clubface—a career six-iron for you—and right into the hazard. Always remember in these situations that one foot too long doesn't do you any good. Ten yards short of the hazard is good, twenty yards short of it is even better. So even though you rarely hit a perfect shot, when you're laying up you have to take into account that *sometimes* you do hit a perfect shot. When you're laying up short of a hazard, play for the ball to finish (not land) ten to twenty yards short of the hazard, and don't forget to factor any roll into the equation. Also, don't forget to factor in the slope of the ground near the hazard. Typically speaking, the ground approaching a water hazard slants toward the hazard, which means the ball is going to run more.

Another mistake players frequently make when laying up is that they don't check the terrain of the landing area they've selected. You don't want to hit what you think is a good layup shot only to find that your approach to the green is from an uphill or sidehill lie. There aren't many things that give the everyday player more trouble than shots from hilly lies. You have to remember that the person who built the course—the architect—was no fool. He knows you might be laying up, so he makes you think about the shot before you play it. Once you've played long enough, one of two things happens: You either get real good at playing from uneven lies, or you get smart about your layup shots. We recommend the second tactic. Another way of looking at this is to forget that old advice about playing one shot at a time and realize that golf is, like billiards, a series of "leaves." The shot you just hit is only as good as the position it *leaves* you in to play the next shot. In match play, you plan at least two shots ahead and sometimes three, depending on the hole and what type of situation your opponent is facing. Even when you are chipping or pitching, you might be trying to hole out but you should always be aware of where you're going to leave the ball. That's not negative thinking—it's smart thinking.

There's a collage of positions that progressively unfolds as you play a hole and you should be thinking about how you're going to get to each position. In a match play, you make a plan for each hole and stick to it until your opponent does something that forces you to modify that plan. Once again, you should ignore that idea of playing the course and not the man. That's a good tactic in stroke play, but in match play you have someone fighting back. You should develop your plan to play the hole in a manner that matches your strengths, and then stay flexible enough to adjust that plan in terms of certain shot selections based on what your opponent has done. So if your opponent hits it in the bushes, instead of going at the green with a five-iron, you might lay up and pitch onto the green and make sure that you make no more than five because he's unlikely to match that score. That's a modification to a plan, unless, of course, you are a lousy wedge player.

In stroke play your opponent isn't paying much attention to what you're doing, but in match play he's watching every move you make. You should be playing to apply the visual pressure of having a ball close to the hole as soon as possible. As such it's probably a good idea to putt the ball whenever you have the opportunity to inside of fifty feet, even when you're not on the green. Almost 75 percent of the time you'll get a putt closer than any chip shot you play, and your worst putt will be about as good as a mediocre chip. When the ball is sitting on the fringe, assuming it's not sitting down, you have more room for error when you putt. If the ball is sitting down, you'll want to play some type of chip, because with the putter you'll probably catch the top half of the ball and it won't go very far.

Once you get outside of fifty feet, putting becomes a more dangerous proposition. The longer the putt gets, the farther back and higher you have to swing the putter, making it difficult to strike the ball solidly and raising the risk of hitting it off center and leaving it six or seven feet short. That isn't awful—you still might make the putt. But your opponent knows you might miss it, too, and that makes him feel like he's still got a chance.

From those longer distances, it's best to chip the ball either with a medium iron such as a six-iron, or become proficient at chipping with a three-wood, which is a shot pioneered by Chi Chi Rodriguez and made popular by Tiger Woods. What those players do is choke down on the three-wood and use a putting stroke. That keeps the head of the three-wood nice and low to the ground and you can hit the ball a pretty fair distance with a short, controlled stroke.

Yardages Hold the Key to Making Smart Safe Shots

Knowing your exact yardage to the hole is vital to playing safe shots, as is recognizing where the trouble lies around the greens. When you know these two things, you can choose the right club for a shot under a given set of circumstances. Think very carefully about your club selection, because even the best swing is going to produce a poor shot if you're using the wrong club.

Your preshot routine starts with establishing your yardage. It doesn't require a lot of time if you know what you're doing. These days, most courses are well marked or provide yardage books. Once you've spotted some sort of yardage marker, you can do one of two things: If you're close enough to it to see it while standing next to your ball, you should be close enough to estimate (within a foot or so) how far you are from the marker. If you're not close enough to see a marker, then find one and pace off the distance between it and your ball. Some players choose to pace off the yardage on every single shot, even if the marker is only five yards ahead of their ball. If you like to do this, we have three pieces of advice for you: Take a caddie, play fast, and play well. Otherwise, someone is liable to hammer you over the head with a six-iron.

On most golf courses, yardages are measured from the middle of a given green to certain points in the fairway (typically 100, 150, and 200 yards), but some courses measure them from the front of the green. If you're playing on an unfamiliar course, be sure to double-check with the starter before you start your round.

Two quite common planning mistakes are to forget to figure the position of the hole into your yardage assessments, and to forget to consider the position of your opponent during club selection. A typical green is approximately thirty yards deep. Assuming you hit your full iron shots at ten-yard intervals, the green is three clubs deep. Here's a fairly common scenario: A player is in the fairway and he sees the 150-yard marker at what he estimates to be ten yards in front of him. There are no hazards short of the green, so he reaches into his bag and yanks out the club he usually uses to hit 160 yards. He goes through his routine, makes a good pass at the ball, and watches as it goes sailing over the flagstick and lands in the middle of the green. The flagstick, of course, was in front of the green. And since the front of the green on almost every green is slanted toward the fairway for drainage, our hero is now faced with a thirty-foot-plus downhill putt. The point is that you must figure out the position of the hole and add or subtract it to your yardage from the middle of the green.

Here's another scenario: Our hero has 160 yards to the middle of the green, which is fronted by a pond. He's learned from his previous mistake and notes that the flag is on the front of the green. Duly noted, he subtracts ten yards from his yardage to arrive at his actual yardage of 150 yards. So he yanks out the club that normally hits 150 yards and makes a decent pass at it, but he catches it just a little fat. Instead of flying 150 yards, it only carries about 143 yards, and splashes into the pond in front of the green. His mistake here was that he planned on perfect execution. He should have planned to hit the ball beyond the hole, not directly to the hole. Had he done that, and adjusted his club selection, he still would have had a good chance of two-putting if he hit the ball pure. Even if he hit the ball fat, it still would have been enough club to carry the water.

Here are some points to consider when determining your actual yardage *and* what club you're going to hit:

- When the hole is in the front of the green, subtract ten yards from the measured yardage to the middle of the green.
- When the hole is in the back of the green, add ten yards to the measured yardage to the middle of the green.
- Not every green is thirty yards deep; that's just an average to use if you don't know for sure. If you can plainly see that the green is deeper than that (or shorter) adjust accordingly.

Watch out for architectural tricks, however! Many of the great architects attempt to deceive you visually by making things appear closer to you than they are. Mounding and bunkers that are short of the green can be tricky. Often there is more distance between them and the front of the green than you can discern. This often leads players to think the distance is shorter than the marked yardage—and that's the trick the designer is trying to play. Trust the yardages! (At Lahinch Golf Club in Ireland, there are several holes that are completely blind, obscured by giant sand dunes. The only guide for a shot is a small white stone on the side of the dune, over which you should play your ball. The stones are moved each day depending on how the hole is playing or where the pin is cut. It's quite unsettling, really, but the caddie whispers to you as you take your club, "Trust the stones." Same goes here. If you're not sure, trust the yardage.)

- If a green is elevated, it affects the distance of your shot. The rule is for every thirty feet of elevation, add ten yards to the measured distance. If this doesn't make sense to you, the easiest way to solidify it in your mind is like this: Imagine that you're hitting from a flat spot to a target that is on the same level as you. Picture the flight of your ball as an arc with a consistent curve. When the landing area for your shot is higher than the area from which you play the shot, the final bit of that arc doesn't exist. Therefore, you need to flatten that arc slightly in your mind, and use a club that will hit the green at the same point where the shorter club would have come to rest on level ground.

- If the green is below where you're playing a shot, reverse the above rule: for every thirty feet of elevation change, subtract ten yards from the measured distance.

- If there is trouble short, especially water, plan to carry the ball at least to the middle of the green, even if the hole is cut in the front of the green. In the same vein, when there is clearly big trouble behind the green (water, trees, desert scrub, etc.), don't attempt to carry the ball all the way back to the hole. To keep it simple: When there is trouble short or long, play for the middle. (We use "middle" in terms of the depth of the green. In terms of width, we'll use "center.")

- If the sides of greens are defended, it's usually by bunkers. When only one side is bunkered, you'll want to favor the opposite side if your opponent is in trouble and the center of the green if you're even with him on that hole. When both sides are bunkered, you should go for the center portion of the green regardless of what your opponent is doing.

- You can divide any green into four quadrants by visualizing two lines, one running the length of the green and one running the width of the green, and crossing in the dead center of the green. In almost any situation, at least one quadrant is going to be safe, i.e., you can play to it with a comfortable margin of error and still be unharmed by a *slightly* misplayed shot. If your opponent is in trouble, you should look for a safe quadrant and play to it. Playing to a safe quadrant might mean an adjustment in club selection. If the safe quadrant is short of the hole, you want to know the yardage to that point, not to the hole.

- If you can do so safely, play to a part of the green that will leave you below or level with the hole. The key word here is "safely." Don't risk hitting the ball in the water just to leave yourself an uphill putt.

- Most high and middle handicappers leave the ball short on approach shots more often than they could care to admit. Only rarely do you see a player of this caliber consistently play approach shots to hole high or even knock it over the green. This bit of insight falls under the category of knowing your own game, because you should never start expecting your opponent to come up short. If you're a middle or high handicapper, you often come up short on approach shots because you seldom hit the ball on the center of the clubface. Remember that you don't have to miss the dead center of the clubface by much to have it adversely affect the length of a shot. If you hit it just a quarter inch off center, that could cost you between ten to twenty yards in distance. (Think about it: The clubface is only about three inches in width, which means if you miss the center by a quarter of an inch, you're one-sixth of the way toward the toe or heel over a very small surface.) Modern, perimeter-weighted designs have improved the quality of the results on off-center hits, but they do more for direction than distance. A perimeter-weighted design is never going to save you in terms of distance. To get the full distance value of any club, you have to hit it dead center—no matter how fancy the material of the clubhead or shaft.

You should factor your tendency to come up short into your yardage/club selection process, especially if you're having a bad day of ball-striking. Think of it as the "miss factor," i.e., if you miss the center of the clubface by a little bit, you're still going to end up where you need to be. This is doubly significant when you're trying to "win ugly." When you're scraping for every edge you can get, admit to yourself that you're playing poorly (but still have a chance to win!) and start thinking more about your club selection.

When you feel as if you're between clubs, i.e., the distance is 145 yards and you hit your seven-iron 150 yards and your eight-iron 140 yards, and there are no hazards to worry about, make the smart choice based on your game. If you're a middle or high handicapper, always take the longer club. If you're a solid low handicapper—like eight or below—then make it based on your swing. If you're a tempo-driven smooth swinger who considers himself a Machine, take the longer club. If you're an attacking, aggressive swinger (a Bomber), go with the shorter club. If you're a low handicapper and you're a Magician, you'll have to make up your own mind, because only you know how you swing.

While you're thinking of all the above, you should also be taking note of your opponent's position. If he's in trouble and has already taken two shots more than you have, you might want to play conservatively when selecting your target area on the green. You'll probably want to go for one of the "safe" quadrants you identified using the tips above, or, if the front of the green is unprotected by hazards, lay up to the front edge and give yourself an easy chip to the hole. If your opponent hits it in the woods and chips out to the fairway, and he gets a handicap stroke on the hole, you have to proceed as if you're even—because you are.

Since you're playing match play, your shot selection is also influenced by your opponent's good play. For instance, if he's away and hits the ball in there pretty tight, you have to respond. If he has a realistic chance at making a birdie, you have a decision to make. If he's not putting well, or you know he doesn't putt well under pressure, then you might want to be thinking that two putts will get you a halve. In that case, you don't want to fire right at the flag, but toward a safe portion of the green from which you feel confident you can get down in two putts. This is a good strategy if his putt is ten feet or longer, since there's just as much of a chance that he'll miss it as there is he'll make it. On the other hand, if he sticks it in there about three feet from the hole, you have to realize there's a high probability he's going to make the putt. So unless you're getting a stroke on the hole or you know this guy is *the* world's worst putter, you've got to try to get the ball somewhere that gives you a realistic attempt at making the putt. If you *are* getting a stroke on the hole, then you've got to play for two putts and the halve. By not doing so, you run a very high risk of giving the hole to him with a misplayed shot that ends up in a bunker or misses a green. If you're *both* getting shots, you revert back to trying to leave yourself a makable putt. It's important to know, however, that leaving yourself a putt you have a chance to make doesn't necessarily mean you have to fire at the flag as if you're trying to hole out. You must have a sense of your own putting skills and feel on a given day, and use that to determine the safest aggressive shot you can play.

Getting Ready to Win Ugly

By the end of the first phase of the match, you should have a pretty good handle on how you're going to play on a given day. Even Tour players admit that the key to being a great player is to score well when you don't have your best stuff—which is more than half the time. When you realize that you are struggling with your game, resign yourself to the fact that you're going to have to win ugly. In other words, don't get caught up in the idea that if you're going to win you have to win by hitting the most stylish shots. There is only one thing about a golf shot that truly matters—where it ends up. There aren't any points awarded for good form in golf. And there's no embarrassment in winning ugly.

So let's assume that after you've warmed up, tried to evaluate your opponent, set the rules, and everything else, you get up on the tee of the first few holes and the ball starts flying sideways on you. It's just going all over the yard. If you want to be a good match player, you have to have a fallback game. Just as in military operations when defensive positions are sometimes prepared to fall back to in case the front is overrun, your fallback game is something you have in reserve for times when things go inexplicably wrong.

The first element of implementing a fallback game is to start getting the ball in play, even if you have to hit irons off the tee. Here's the definition of golfing insanity: You find that something isn't working and you keep doing it. How many times do you have to pump the driver into the bushes before you realize you're going to lose? If you're playing a 420-yard par four and you have to play two five-irons and a wedge to reach the green, do it! At least you'll have a putt for par and a chance to hang in the hole. If you can keep the ball in play off the tee, you've got a chance against anybody. So the first move you make is to stick that driver back in the bag and start hitting fairway woods or irons from the tee. When you're hitting the ball wildly off-line, you can't worry about keeping up with your opponent in terms of distance. Sometimes dropping back to more lofted clubs is enough to get you back on track.

If you try hitting fairway woods and irons from the tee and it has little or no effect on your downward spiral, then it's time to go to your fallback swing. If you don't have a fallback swing, you should develop one. The easiest type of fallback swing is one that produces a weak cut shot that curves from left to right, but not so much that it will get you in trouble. This swing feels as if you're "blocking" the ball out onto the fairway with a swing that is almost entirely an arm swing with very little wrist action. In the final round of the 1988 U.S. Open, Curtis Strange, the eventual champion, went to just such a strategy because he felt his game was off that day. He realized that if he could just keep the ball in the fairway he'd still have a chance. (Strange eventually won an eighteen-hole play-off versus Nick Faldo.) Here are the basics for playing that cut shot: Set up with your body (feet, knees, and hips) aimed left of your target. Aim your clubface left of your target, too, but not quite as much as your body—split the difference. When you swing, don't worry about trying to create power—don't reach to try to make the longest possible backswing. In fact, you should feel as if your backswing is shorter than usual. Swing the club along the lines of your body and follow through completely, just like you normally would but with one exception: Through the impact zone you should feel as if you're "holding on" to the club, and pushing the face squarely down the target line for as long as possible. Imagine that you're trying to keep the toe of the club from rolling over and passing the heel of the club. The shot produced won't be exceptionally powerful, but you should be able to predict the ball flight with some degree of consistency. Two final points to remember about the fallback cut shot: The ball isn't going to run very much when it hits the ground, so select your targets accordingly. Also, you won't carry the ball as far as you typically do with each club. So make the proper adjustments in club selection. Having that fallback cut shot in your game can help you win ugly, but it's something you should work out on the practice tee before using it in competition. (One final note: We assume you're smart enough to know that "fallback" in this sense doesn't mean to fall back from the ball while you're swinging.)

To Give or Not to Give? Is It a Question at All?

Earlier in this chapter, we talked about the idea of possibly giving a few putts early in the match in order to prevent your opponent from getting in a groove with his putter. Not all players agree with this strategy. Two things determine whether it's a good move or not: the type of match you're playing and what type of opponent you're up against.

Every golfer has heard about how Gene Sarazen or Walter Hagen would give their opponent putts all day long until the last couple of holes and then make them putt everything out. This seems like a good strategy, but you have to realize that those guys were world-class players. If you are in any match that you don't consider friendly, and your sole purpose is to win, then make the guy putt everything. In fact, you can even announce on the first tee, "Putt everything out." If you're playing against a fine player and he knocks it within three inches of the hole, then go ahead and knock it away. But if you're playing a middle or high handicapper, make them putt everything two feet or longer. All it takes is for one of your opponents to miss one of those short ones he's expecting you to concede and, brother, he'll be a basket case the rest of the day worrying about whether he's going to make one or not. This is especially true on Bermuda greens, which are very slow and unpredictable.

Another time you never want to give any putts is during the

early phases of afternoon matches. You might think, "Ah, hell, it's just the beginning," but the golf course doesn't know that. The course has been played on all morning long, so the green has already taken a beating. And the grass is growing longer, which is going to slow them down. When the everyday player misses a putt, it's typically because he leaves the ball short of the hole. This is because the prevailing tendency among amateurs (especially high handicappers) is to slow down the putterhead through impact. This is sometimes referred to as "deceleration," and the net result is a putt that is short and off-line. It follows, then, that the slower the greens the more likely these guys are to miss the short putts.

The later in the day it gets, the more you start to see the effects of what we'll call the "donut effect," which means the hole gets "raised" from people bending over and picking the ball out of the hole. What really happens is that the area around the hole gets pressed down from the weight of the players, creating a difficult-to-detect dip as the ball moves close to the hole. If a putt isn't hit firmly enough to make it dead center, the ball might not go in.

So, should you ever give a putt you think the other guy might miss? Only consider it under the circumstances described earlier in the chapter, namely, when you have a short uphill putt you *know* you're going to make, and you think it might work out to your advantage a few holes later if your opponent hasn't had a short tester. The benefit of this strategy is short-lived because your opponent assumes you're not going to give him putts late in the round. So if you're going to try this, your best chance of making it pay off is to make him putt one within the next two or three holes—preferably the very next hole.

Keep an Eye Out for Skulduggery

Far be it for the authors to suggest that your opponent is a cheater. Let's just say that there's no law that only choir boys can play golf. If your opponent is going to try to cheat, he's probably not going to do it in the early phases of the match. Like any good cheater, he'll use those early holes to build a little trust factor and make you think he's a good guy—maybe even give you a putt when you're not expecting him to do so. It's in this second phase of the match that you might start to see some shenanigans.

By and large, cheaters aren't stupid, so they're not going to try stuff such as saying they made a three on the hole when they've actually made a five and know you were watching every move they made. They'll try to get you by nickel and diming you on the greens.

Keep an eye on your opponent when he marks his ball on the green. You might think that an inch or two won't make a difference, but it does if they have to putt over a spike mark or an old pitch mark in the green. Make sure that your opponent places the ball back properly, i.e., if he places the coin directly behind the ball, don't let him get away with placing the ball back *next* to the coin—that quarter of an inch could give him a clearer line to the hole. Another trick to watch for occurs when your opponent marks the ball by placing the coin in front of the ball, then places the ball in front of the coin when he puts it back down. This move makes his putt shorter by a few turns of the ball, and sometimes that's all it takes.

Here's another sneaky trick: If your putt is going to travel on a line over where your opponent has marked his ball, it is customary for him to move his marker. This is done by lining up the head of the putter with a landmark and moving the coin a clubhead's length on a line with that landmark. Some players will try to take advantage of this when re-marking the ball by moving the mark closer to the hole than the original mark. They do this by pointing the clubhead at something other than their landmark, causing the heel of the club to swing closer to the hole. So before you get absorbed in your own putt, make sure you have an idea of the line your opponent is using as a reference.

It's also a good idea to watch closely any gardening your

opponent decides to do on the green. Fixing a pitch mark made by a ball—no matter how long it has been there—is always permitted, even if your ball isn't on the green. What is *not* legal is to fix or tap down spike marks on the green, or to rip out little pieces of grass if they are still attached to the earth, i.e., they're still growing. A sly move a lot of cheaters try is to start digging up around a spike mark before you look at it, claiming it was a pitch mark. If you catch your opponent doing this, he loses the hole. (On a related matter, you might not be aware that it *is* legal to fix old hole positions on the green. So if you have to roll a putt over an old hole location, you can dig up and tamp down those edges. The greenkeeper might not be too thrilled about it, but it's legal.)

Getting Ready: The Day of the Match

The player who wins a match is usually the one who is best prepared to win. On the day of a match, there's a long list of things you must do in order to prep yourself for competition. The list begins with preparing your body.

Stretching and preparing your body. Golf is not the most physically demanding sport, but it does place some demands on your body. When your body isn't ready to perform, it doesn't. So, before you warm up on the practice tee, warm up your body. Here's a five-minute stretching routine that anyone can do. As with any stretching, this routine is best done *slowly* and *carefully*.

1. Turn your head to the right, looking as far over your shoulder as possible. Take your left hand and push gently against the left side of your face, nudging the stretch a little farther. (Remember, this is a *gentle* push. Don't hurt yourself.) Hold this position for ten to fifteen seconds, then switch sides and repeat. Do each side three times.

2. Reach across your body with your left arm and grab the

back of your right elbow with your left hand. Now, stretch your right arm across your body, placing it under your chin if that's possible. Hold it ten seconds, then do it to the other side. Repeat each side three times.

3. Clasp your hands behind your back, and raise your arms up and out. Repeat three times.

4. Bend forward, gently, from your waist and grasp your ankles. If you need to flex your knees to do so, that's okay. Let your neck and arms relax as you bend slowly forward from your hips. While you're still holding onto your ankles, straighten your knees until you feel a comfortable stretch in the backs of your legs. Hold this for ten to fifteen seconds, then let go of your ankles and *slowly* raise yourself up, bending your knees as you straighten your trunk. Repeat three times.

5. Stand with your back up against a tree or a golf cart. Rotate your body to the right, so you can grab ahold of the tree or cart with both hands without moving your feet. Look over your left shoulder as you do this. You can increase the tension by pulling yourself around a little farther with your hands. Hold for ten to fifteen seconds, then repeat with the other side. Repeat with both sides three times.

6. Stand with your feet shoulder-width apart and raise your right arm above your head. Keeping your knees slightly flexed, lean to your left and slide your left hand down the outside of your left thigh to just above your knee. You should feel a comfortable stretch along the left side of your torso. Hold it ten to fifteen seconds, then switch to the other side. Repeat three times.

Getting the most out of your body involves more than just stretching. You should also drink plenty of water before and during the match. Most people don't drink enough water as it is, but when you're feeling pressure you'll start to feel that dehydration more than you normally do. (If you play in the desert or extremely hot temperatures, you might already know this, but it doesn't hurt to point it out:

You should be drinking water throughout your round. Take a few sips on every hole, because in the desert or low humidity places you may not sweat very much, but you are nonetheless becoming dehydrated. If you play in Florida, the fact that your shirt is soaked with sweat should remind you to drink up.) As far as the water is concerned, it's probably a good idea to toss a few bottles of water into your bag or cart, because the pond water they put in the coolers out on the course isn't that great.

Before you start (and when you make the turn), don't eat a lot of heavy, greasy food. The last thing you want is to have that greasy food make you bloated or lethargic or both. We suggest that you stick to fruit until after the match is over. Fruit will provide you with energy and won't weigh you down. You can even throw a few bananas or apples in your bag. (If you want to get real serious, slice the apples up before the round and put them in a zip-lock-type bag. That way it won't be as messy when you eat it on the course.)

Everyone knows people who are seemingly incapable of properly functioning without a few cups of coffee in the morning. If you feel as if you need a cup in the morning to calm your nerves, drink just enough to calm you down, but don't drink too much. If you overdo the coffee, you'll get jittery out on the course when that excess caffeine kicks in (or when it wears off). Coffee also promotes dehydration—it's a natural diuretic.

Finally, on the subject of keeping your body and mind sharp, wait until you finish your match before you drink any alcohol. If you honestly don't care whether you win, then it really doesn't matter, does it? In that case, we simply ask that you save one for us.

Working the Practice Tee

After you're done stretching, head to the practice tee. (Better yet, stretch while you're at the practice tee.) Take a middle iron out of your bag and start swinging slowly back and forth over and over without stopping. You're not hitting a ball during this, but just trying to get loose. Keep doing this for a minute or so. If your body feels as if it will allow it, each time you swing, stretch a little farther into the backswing and follow through.

Begin your actual ball-striking warm-up by hitting three or four twenty-yard wedge shots. Then hit a series of three-ball sets—still with the wedge—in increasing ten-yard increments. Don't worry about making pure contact. However, if you find the notion of hitting the ball fat a few times a bit disconcerting, tee up each ball.

When you're warming up, remember what you're trying to accomplish—a warm-up of your body and your feel for the club. Don't turn a warm-up into swing-reconstruction surgery five minutes before you head for the tee. The time to work hard on your swing is *after* a round or on days you're not playing.

Some players like to "cruise" the opponent on the practice tee prior to the beginning of a match. If you do this, you have to exercise some caution. A guy can swing like an old lady beating off a mugger with an umbrella and still be a pretty good player, but that's fairly uncommon. Check out his swing to see if it looks fundamentally sound—like it will hold up all day. If so, you should expect him to be a pretty good player and that you're going to have a fight on your hands. The two most important things you'll be able to pick up watching him on the range are his ball-flight tendencies and general approach to the game. You'll be able to tell the Bomber because he'll be hammering that driver for a good while when he's warming up. The Machine will be going through his routine before every practice ball he hits, and will take some time between balls. The Magician will be flipping little wedge shots more frequently than the other players on the practice range.

Preparing Your Short Game

Nothing is more discouraging to your opponent than your suddenly getting up and down from a garbage can to tie him when he thinks he has you beaten. And then, on the next hole, you do the same thing. And so on. A sharp short game is one of the most deadly psychological weapons you can employ in match play. It's a good idea to get your short game cranked up before heading out to the course. You should spend some time playing chips and pitches to a practice green, and getting your feel for the sand in a practice bunker. Even though you know how to do these things, every new round of golf brings a new feel with it—the ball always feels different on the clubhead than it did the day before. When you're practicing the chips, pitches, and bunker shots, focus on a spot where you want to land the ball, just like you would on the course.

With your practice putts, you want to work on two things just before you head to the first tee: short putts and real long putts. Gary Player used to talk about how right before he'd tee off he'd make a series of one-foot putts just to ingrain in his mind the image of the ball going into the hole. You might try that, or if not, make sure you spend a few minutes banging in two- and three-footers, focusing on two things. First, make sure you maintain the speed of the clubhead through the contact zone. More short putts are missed because of a decelerating clubhead than for any other reason. (If you need to feel that you're speeding up the clubhead to accomplish this, go for it. You don't really want to accelerate through the ball either, but if that image works for you, use it.) Second, when you visualize the line to the hole, see the line as wide as the hole itself—it's amazing how well this works. (Another thing you can try on short putts is something Johnny Miller used to do. Once you get the club set behind the ball, look at the hole throughout your entire stroke, and feel the clubhead push the ball toward the hole. All you'll see is the ball going into the hole. This helps remove any chance that you'll look up too quickly—a primary cause of decelerating the putter.)

You also want to be certain you get some long putts under your hat before moving to the first tee. How well you perform in match play will be determined in large part by how consistent you are at getting the long putts close to the hole. Long putts are all about feel, and if you want to win in match play, you have to throw out that old idea about getting the ball inside a four-foot circle around the hole, because if you leave yourself enough four-footers you're eventually going to miss one. There is one tried-and-true method of getting a feel for the length of the stroke required for any long putt that will travel over fairly flat terrain. While standing over the ball, swing your right arm back and forth as if you were going to roll the ball to the hole using a low toss—almost as if you were bowling. If you have even the most basic sense of hand-to-eye coordination, your brain will figure out how far back and through you need to move your arm. That's the same length stroke you should put on the ball—back and through. (Don't forget the "through" part; it's important!) For downhill putts, move closer to the hole while making your pretend tosses. For uphill putts, move farther away from the hole to make your imaginary tosses. Finally, on long putts, pick an exact spot where you would like the ball to finish and zone in on it. It should be close enough to the hole that it leaves you a tap-in—preferably an uphill one.

So, you made it to the first tee. Congratulations. Now that you have your body loose, keep it that way. Keep moving around, slowly walking or doing some mild stretching. Whatever you do, don't sit down and let your muscles tighten up again. It's also time for one last equipment check. Check your bag to see that you have no more than fourteen clubs, especially if you own more than fourteen clubs and you switch them around. It's funny how clubs can end up in your bag, and they don't have to be put there by you. Sometimes there are mix-ups when your clubs are being cleaned by a cart attendant or a caddie. When you're counting, make sure that you take the woods out of the bag so your headcovers don't obscure your view of the bag. Check. Place a distinguishing mark on any ball that you might put into play, and make certain you tell your opponent the brand and model of ball you'll be playing *and* show him your identifying mark.

MASTERS OF MATCH PLAY:
WALTER HAGEN

Bobby Jones and Walter Hagen met only once in a head-to-head match. See if you can guess who won by reading the following quote from Jones, spoken directly after the match: "When a man misses his drive, then misses his second shot, and wins with a birdie, it just gets my goat!" Hagen, of course, won that match and a whole bunch of others—he won five PGA Championships at match play (1921, 1924, 1925, 1926, 1927), and each match in those wins was a thirty-six-holer. Only Jack Nicklaus has won as many PGA Championships (all at stroke play), but Hagen alone holds these PGA Championship records: most finals (6), most semifinals (8), most consecutive finals (5), most consecutive matches won (22), and lowest medalist score (140 in 1926) to go on to win the championship. He also had the second-highest qualifying score (151 in 1925) of any eventual champion. His career record in the PGA Championship was 40-10, and when he lost he didn't go down easy. In 1932 it took John Golden forty-three holes to beat Hagen in a match scheduled for thirty-six holes.

Hagen was a giant figure in the history of the game. Along with his five PGA Championships he had four British Open titles and two U.S. Opens (the first in 1914, the year after Francis Ouimet's colossal victory in that same event), and was a central figure in the first six Ryder Cups. During those Cups (1927–1937) he served as the playing United States captain in the first five, compiling a 7-1-1 record. In 1937 he was captain again, but did not play in the contest. His involvement in the Ryder Cup was fitting—Hagen had helped pave the way for golf professionals in the world of golf. Before Hagen, professionals were regarded socially beneath the country club set. Hagen's skills and personality helped to change that.

More than anything else, Hagen was known for his seemingly breezy attitude toward the game. He is often attributed with the saying, "Never hurry, never worry, and always take time to smell the flowers along the way." Indeed, Hagen was the James Bond of golf—he always got his man, but did so in such an effortless fashion that it disarmed his opponents. Which was exactly his goal—when Hagen was *beginning* to get under your skin, you didn't notice it. When he had *finished* getting under your skin, it was too late to do anything about it. More than anything, Hagen proved that you could be a serious competitor without being overly serious about yourself.

What you can learn from the Haig

Hagen was one of the premier swingers of the club during his time, a fact that might not be readily obvious to you if you've ever seen his swing in old motion pictures. Like a lot of players of his time, Hagen appeared to move around a lot while swinging the club, giving the impression of what might be called a "loose" swing. (That he had active feet during his preswing setup and the fact that old movies made almost everyone's swing look herky-jerky lent some fuel to this notion.) In truth, Hagen had a fairly controlled swing.

One thing that Hagen did extraordinarily well was make the transition from backswing to downswing. From his unusually wide stance (which he might have picked up as a wannabe pro baseball player), Hagen initiated the downswing with his lower body before his hands had reached their finished position at the top of his backswing. These simultaneous movements made it seem as if Hagen was swaying laterally away from the ball (considered a modern-day no-no). By starting your downswing from the ground up—using your hips and legs before your arms—you can achieve the same powerful downswing as Hagen did. To accomplish this, start your downswing by aggressively turning your hips toward the target. This will set in motion the delayed reaction that allows the club to pause for a moment at the top before whipping down to catch up with your lower body (gaining speed all the while). The result is pure power.

What about that notorious Hagen sway? A close look at his swing in old movies reveals that Hagen's head was stock-still *and* behind the ball until well after impact—a commonality among all great ball strikers.

If all your balls aren't the same brand, it's no big deal—just mark them all the same and show your opponent your mark. To mark the ball, use a waterproof marking pen. You don't have to re-create the ceiling of the Sistine Chapel on your ball—a dot or two in a consistent spot and pattern will do the trick. Check. Make sure you have a towel with you. Check. (If you have a caddie, make sure he has a towel with him.) If you're on an unfamiliar course, make sure you've checked with the pro or the starter to confirm the location of the yardage markers *and* that they are measured to the center of the green. Check. Is it sunny and warm? Make sure you have bottled water and nongreasy sunscreen with you. Check. Look like it might rain? Make sure you have a rain jacket in your bag *and* extra towels stored in a plastic bag. Take a separate plastic bag to store wet towels. Check. Umbrella. Check. If you wear a glove, have at least one extra. Check. (If it starts to rain, hang the towel from the inside of the umbrella to keep it dry. Do the same with your glove between shots, using the Velcro fastener.) Check. Make sure you have two or three coins in your pocket. It's an awkward moment if you reach into your pocket on the first green to get a coin to mark your ball and realize you don't have a marker. That will create some inner tension and that leads to stress, which is not a good thing early in a match. It's a little thing, but it helps. Also you can get those coins jingling at a pretty good pace in your pocket, which may or may not unnerve your opponent. We don't recommend that you do that, but you can make your own decisions.

4

Going for the Kill

Winning a close match often comes down to creating an unexpected edge for yourself. If that sounds a little distasteful to you consider this story. Ben Hogan's home course was Shady Oaks in Fort Worth, Texas. He got so sick and tired of losing matches to the other guys (because he had to give them so many shots) that he resorted to some trickery to win. One morning, Hogan had the greenkeeper go out and cut all the hole positions in the front left portion of the green. Hogan knew amateurs typically don't take enough club for a shot, and that if they came up short on a front pin they wouldn't be on the green at all, and they'd have to chip or pitch. Hogan also knew that the average player typically cuts the ball from left to right, so that it's tough for them to stick it tight to a left pin position. Like all good players, Hogan could move the ball either way, so he could easily draw the ball into those left pins. After having the course set up like that, Hogan made the biggest bets he could with any takers, and, of course, went out and drilled them. This might be an extreme example of trying to gain an edge, but the point is that in match play you have to take any edge you can get.

Down the Stretch: The Pressure Builds

Even in the most meaningless of matches, there is some degree of intensity. People hate to lose. More specifically, people hate to fail—they despise being put in a position where they seemingly can control the outcome and fail to live up to their own expectations. Unless you're playing a real cupcake (or, on the downside, you're being obliterated), the intensity of the pressure in match play starts to build toward a crescendo over the last six holes. When you hit the thirteenth tee, it's time to pull up your bootstraps—it's kill or be killed.

When the pressure is on, it should help you to realize that you're not the only one feeling it—the other guy is, too. Your goal is to lessen the pressure on yourself while turning it up on your opponent. Decreasing your self-pressure is something you do in your head. Increasing the pressure on your opponent is something you do with your clubs. Remember the Oscar-winning movie *Braveheart*? Early on in that picture, the young William Wallace is staring at the sword of his uncle, Argyle, and vengeful thoughts are racing through his mind. He's dreaming of the day he can avenge the murder of his father and brother. Argyle notices this and says, "First, you learn to use this," and he taps the boy's forehead. "Then, I'll teach you to use this," says Argyle, brandishing the sword. That is a perfect description of the mind-set you need to have over the closing holes of a match.

Mastering Yourself

There are some players who thrive on pressure. At the highest level of the game, the best players all do. But you don't have to search the PGA Tour to find players who excel under the gun. We all know guys who are great money players—players who seem to sort of hang around until a match reaches the point when it's going to be decided. Then they somehow ratchet their game up an extra level and win the match. It's almost as if they really weren't trying their hardest for most of the match, but that's not actually the case. The truth is, players like that play *better* than their normal game when something is on the line. They know that if they focus and don't make any mistakes, their opponent is bound to make at least one mistake. And when it's crunch time, all it takes is one mistake to determine the outcome of a match.

Maybe you're one of the lucky ones who has a knack for pulling it all together in the clutch. And maybe you're not. On the off chance that you're not, here's how the "money" players keep a grip on themselves as they head down the stretch. Learn to embrace these ideas, and you'll have accomplished the first part of finishing off an opponent.

1. They understand *what* pressure is. You know that pressure can manifest itself in any form in any phase of your life—work, home, relationships. Most people instinctively begin to rush, to "press," when they feel pressure. After all, what is pressure? In a match, is it worrying about something simple, such as forgetting how to swing the club? Of course not—you're not going to forget how to swing the club. Pressure happens when you fret over the outcome. It's the waiting that gets to people. They can't take the waiting, so they rush things in an attempt to bring a resolution to the situation quickly. They just want it to end, and bringing the situation to a hasty conclusion takes on more importance than bringing it to a successful one. That is not how great match players think. They realize the end of the match is the longest part of the match, and that it cannot be rushed. They also know that in all likelihood their opponent *is* rushing, and panicking, and sweating. . . .

2. They treat pressure as their comfort zone. The best pressure player in the history of the game was Jack Nicklaus. He possessed a quality that all great match players share: He felt *at home* under pressure. He knew that pressure would get caught in the throats of the guys he played against, and instead of viewing it as something to be loathed, Nicklaus viewed pressure as the golden gate to his goals—the more the other guys choked, the greater his chance of winning. When you're in a match and you can feel the pressure, you should realize your chances of winning aren't decreasing, *they're increasing,* right along with the chances of your opponent folding up his tent.

3. They stick to their routine. We've already established that when the heat is on, players instinctively try to speed the proceedings along. You're not going to do this. Once you've acknowledged the pressure exists and that you can use it to your benefit, you have to reinforce your focus. The longest part of playing any shot is the preshot routine, especially because you're not actively moving the game along as you go through it. It's the preshot routine—and therefore the vital aim and alignment points of the swing—that are most typically rushed by players who are choking. The next time you're under pressure, tell yourself you're going to go through your preshot routine slower and more precisely than ever. The best way to accomplish this is to talk yourself through it in your mind as follows:

—From behind the ball, select a target, factoring in the combined carry and roll of the ball when selecting a club.

—While still behind the ball, elect an intermediate target two to ten feet ahead of you on the target line. An old divot, twig, or discolored patch of grass will do.

—After approaching the ball, step into your setup with your right foot first, keeping your body open to the target. Set the club behind the ball and aim the lead edge perpendicular to that old divot (or whatever you chose as your intermediate target).

—Set your left foot so that both feet are parallel to the target line. Do the same with your shoulders.

—When you look up at your target, make sure you see it clearly. If it appears that you're looking over your left shoulder at it, you may have set your body closed of (aimed right of) your target. If that's the case, back off and start over.

—Focus on a swing key.

4. They have a swing key. A swing key is like a mantra, a simple thought that you can repeat to yourself as you stand over a shot to focus on making a good swing without excessively cluttering your mind. Here are some situation-oriented swing keys you can use under pressure.

—*On the tee*. One word: *Tempo*. "I'm going to swing this club back and through at the same pace. I'm not going to quit on it and I'm not going to rush it through impact. *Tempo*."

—*With a long iron or fairway wood*. Two words: *Light* and *long*. "I'm going to grip this club as lightly as possible, and I'm going to make a long, low take-away. *Light and long*."

—*An iron from the rough*. Two words: *Back* and *open*. "I'm going to play this ball slightly back in my stance [from its normal position] and I'm going to open the clubface slightly at address. When I hit it, it's going to slide a little right, and run a little more than normal. *Back and open*."

—*A shot from a fairway bunker*. One word: *Quiet*. "I'm going to dig my feet in, choke up on the grip one inch, and make my backswing using only my arms. My lower body will be quiet. *Quiet*."

—*From a greenside bunker*. One word: *Finish*. "I'm going to pick my spot where I want the club to enter the sand, then I'm going to make sure I finish my swing with a complete follow-through. *Finish*."

—**On a chip or pitch.** Two words: *Steady head.* "I'm going to pick my landing area, figure out during my practice swing how hard I have to swing to carry the ball there, then I'm going to lock my head down and keep it steady for a count of two after impact. *Steady head.*"

—**On a long putt.** Two words: *Feel it.* "I'm going to determine how long my stroke should feel by pretending I'm rolling the ball to the hole. Then I'm just going to feel it happen. *Feel it.*"

—**On a short putt.** Three words: *Head to hole,* or *head to target.* "I'm going to make sure I push the putterhead through toward my target, which is the point at the top of the break. If there is no break and the target is the hole, then I'm going to push the putterhead through the ball and toward the hole. *Head to target. Head to hole.*"

5. They always know how their opponent stands. That's pretty simple. If you don't know, ask. Your opponent must tell you. If he doesn't, he loses the hole.

6. They know the Rules, and know how to use them to their advantage. Another simple one. There's an entire chapter on the Rules later in this book.

7. When they're not comfortable over a shot, they back off and get reset. If you're in a match and you feel uncomfortable standing over a big shot, *don't swing.* Back off and go through your preshot routine until you feel confident about the shot.

8. They know the power of adrenaline. In the 1989 British Open at Royal Troon, Mark Calcavecchia, Wayne Grady, and Greg Norman were in a four-hole play-off for the title. On the final hole, Norman, who was in position to win, hit the same club off the tee that he'd hit in the regulation round. In regulation, his drive ended up fine. In the play-off, it ended up in a hideous pot bunker—a bunker he felt certain he couldn't reach with his chosen club. What happened? He was pumped. The adrenaline was gushing through him like a Texas oil well, and he hammered that drive right into the bunker. Believe it or not, when you're playing in a match in your club championship, you're every bit as jacked up as Greg Norman was during that British Open, so make the adjustment. If you feel pumped, it's worth a club in distance—maybe two if the ground is hard.

9. They're not lazy. If a match is tight, and a good match player needs information about where the hole is cut or something similar, he'll walk up until he can see it. If you need information, go get it. If you find you have the wrong club, and your cart is back across the fairway, go back and get the right club. Winning is hard enough without erecting your own barriers.

You've Learned to Use Your Mind, Now Use Your Weapons

So, you finally made it. There you are on the fourteenth fairway, Sunday afternoon, finals of the Old Oak Fence Golf Links Club Championship. It's time to grind, so here's what you need to know about the shots you're going to play as you head for the clubhouse and that big celebration in the bar.

Does First on Win?

There has always been some question about whether or not you should purposely play short of your opponent from the tee of a par four in order to make sure you play first to the green. There's an equally old saying that says, "First on wins," meaning the first player to get his ball on the green will win the hole. Does it hold water? The answer depends on what kind of player you are. If you're a Machine and you're playing a Bomber, the answer is yes, first on is going to win a lot of holes for you. The reason for this is that once you're on the green, the Bomber is going to feel the heat and think he's got to get it inside you. His nature is such that

GREAT MOMENTS IN THE RYDER CUP:
1975, NICKLAUS GETS BEAT BY A GUY WEARING SHORTS—TWICE!

This little story may teach you more than anything else in this book. In 1975, Jack Nicklaus was the absolute king of the golf universe. For sure, Johnny Miller had made a lot of noise by winning a bunch of Tour events and the 1973 U.S. Open, but Nicklaus had nipped this challenge to his superiority in the bud by winning the 1975 Masters and PGA Championship. He arrived at Laurel Valley Golf Club in Pennsylvania as the playing linchpin of an awesome American team captained by Arnold Palmer, and including Hale Irwin, Lee Trevino, Bob Murphy, Lou Graham, Gene Littler, Billy Casper, Al Geiberger, Tom Weiskopf, Johnny Miller, J. C. Snead, and Raymond Floyd.

The Cup itself was a snooze—the Americans crushed the Great Britain and Ireland team, just as everyone had expected. In fact the only

he might do just that and hit it stiff, but he also may hit his eight-iron thirty yards off-line and into the trees. So, in the case of Machine versus Bomber, "first on wins" is a good strategy for the Machine, because par is going to beat the Bomber on a few holes toward the end of the round. (As a side note, the Machine isn't going to have to lay back off the tee—the Bomber is going to out-drive him regardless of what club he hits.) In the case of the Machine versus the Magician, it's a pick 'em. If the Machine simply opts to get it *anywhere* on the green, the Magician is still thinking he can halve the hole. If he does it enough times as the holes run out, the Machine may start to doubt himself. In a matchup of Bomber versus Magician, anything goes.

Regarding the specific notion of laying back, the only player who really has a big decision to make is the Bomber. Should he lay back to give himself first crack at the green? No way. First, it rules out his intimidation factor. Second, it puts him in a spot he's not used to playing.

thing of note to happen that week in September was that the mighty Nicklaus lost two singles matches in the same day to Brian Barnes, who up until that point in Ryder Cup singles play was 2–4 on his career and had never won a major championship.

It was certainly an odd sight when Barnes showed up for his morning match with Nicklaus wearing shorts and puffing on a pipe. Shorts! It just isn't done in professional golf. Nevertheless, Barnes went out and hammered Nicklaus, 4 and 2. Now the Bear most certainly had his back up. The ultimate match-play hybrid, perhaps the only Bomber/Machine in history, couldn't possibly lose to a pipe-smoking wearer of Bermuda shorts! Fate offered Nicklaus his opportunity to correct this fluke by matching him up against Barnes once again in the afternoon singles. (The two-singles-matches-in-one-day format has long since been abandoned.) The good-humored Barnes proceeded to dust Nicklaus again, 2 and 1. The moral of the story? Don't take any opponent lightly.

What if you're playing against the same type of player as yourself? Should you lay back then? If you're having a good day hitting your irons, it's a good strategy to consider on *one or two holes.* Maybe you can catch your man by surprise. If you decide to do this, hit your tee shot to a point where you'll be playing a favorite iron into the green.

Stay Out of the Divots

Now that we may have talked you out of laying back off the tee, here's a reason you might consider it if, in terms of driving distance, you're about average. The later in the day it gets, the more divots there will be in the landing area. So unless you're a Bomber and you're going to fly it forty yards past where everyone else landed, you may want to lay back off the tee to make sure you get a clean lie in the fairway. Driving the ball into a divot may well have cost Payne Stewart the 1998 U.S. Open. When it happened to him late in the final round, he hit a poor shot and opened the door for Lee Janzen.

Play Smart Approaches Late in the Day

No part of the golf course takes a bigger pounding than the greens, and no part of the green takes a bigger pounding than the area right around the hole. The area around the hole is the only place where *every* player treads on ground that can directly affect your shot. So what does all of this mean to you? If you play in the early morning, not that much. If you play late in the morning and into the afternoon, or your entire match is in the afternoon, it means quite a bit, especially on a dry day.

Unless the green has been hit by rain during the day, two things are happening: It is getting firmer and the grass is growing longer. The grass-getting-longer part is easy to figure out—your putts will be a little bit slower than they were at the beginning of your round.

You must account for the greens getting harder as you plan your approach shots. First off, since the greens are harder, you'll want to consider playing your approaches to the front of the green, particularly if you're playing a two-piece ball. If you fly the ball into the middle of the green or the back, there's a chance it could bounce over the green.

The firmness of the greens also affects the specific spot on the green you select as your target. Since the firmest part of any green will be the area right around the hole, you probably shouldn't play a shot to land right next to the hole. If you do, and you execute the shot, you might watch in horror as the ball ricochets off the green like a super ball off a turnpike. Instead, pick a side and play a little left of the hole or a little right of the hole, outside of the circle where people have been walking all day. The area to the sides of the hole won't be as densely packed down from the body weight of the players who preceded you, since the farther you get from the hole the more dispersed those players will have been.

Make Adjustments in the Sand

The sand in the bunkers is probably drying out faster than any other feature of the golf course. The drier the sand gets, the looser it gets and the easier the club slides through it. This increases the odds of hitting the ball heavy out of the sand. So when the sand is dry and loose, dig in a little deeper and stand a little farther away from the ball. This will shallow out your swing plane and let you hit a little closer to the ball without losing control of the shot. The ball will go a little higher, however, so adjust for that.

Be Smarter Than the Other Guy in the Short Game

One of the great debates in golf has always been whether you should leave the flagstick in the hole or take it out when you feel as if you have a chance to hole out from off the green. You have the option to do either, and late in the match it can be a big decision. Here's the best way to look at it: If you hit the shot perfectly, it's going to go in the hole whether the flagstick is in or out. If you hit the ball short, it's not going to go in the hole no matter what. If you hit the ball too hard the flagstick has a chance to save you. As a general rule, when you're chipping or putting downhill from off the green, leave the pin in the hole, because there's a good chance you'll hit the shot with too much force. If the ball hits the flagstick squarely, it might drop in. On uphill shots, you're more likely to leave the ball short. Therefore, if the ball gets to the hole at all it will be moving pretty slow. So if it makes you more comfortable, take the flagstick out when you're going uphill toward the hole.

Don't Finish Out on the Green

After you've putted the ball up near the hole, you may be tempted to hit the next putt and finish out your hole. First, you have to re-member that if you're not away, it's not your turn to play. So if you want to finish out and you're not away, you have to ask your opponent, "Is it okay if I finish out?" It's entirely up to him. The question, however, is do you *want* to finish out?

Often on television during the Ryder Cup or other match-play event, a player will finish out and the announcers will say something like, "Smart move there by Freddie to finish out. Now all the pressure is on Jose." Was it really a smart move by Freddie? Probably not. Golf is a game of information, both given and received. If you elect to finish out putting while your opponent still has some putting to do, you're giving away information. If your opponent's putt is going to run along your line, he can see exactly how it's going to break and at what speed it should be moving. Even if he's not on your line, he can get information about the speed of the green in general around the hole, and the overall break around the hole. The other factor to think about is that you're showing your hand before you have to. Once every so often you're going to miss one of those putts, and when you do you give your opponent a free run at the hole. There's no point in taking the guesswork out of the hole for your opponent. If they don't know for sure, they have to proceed as if you're going to make the putt. This probably means they'll be less aggressive in trying to make their own. If you're playing a high handicapper, he's probably going to miss his putt anyway, so why would you step up there trying to put pressure on someone who's probably already psyching himself out? Besides, there's more for him to think about if you haven't holed out, and that makes it less likely he'll focus on the task at hand. Overall, we think the notion of "finishing out" is a bad strategy. You put pressure on yourself and quite often, unless you really know what you are doing, you hurry and you miss the putt. Our suggestion is to mark the ball and let the opponent show *you* something. Let him show *his* hand. You might even suggest that he finish out. Something sort of casual like, "You can go ahead and finish out if you like." More often than not he will attempt to do so. If he misses, you're in fat city.

And if he makes it, you've gained information *and* you know what score you need to make.

Your Man Will Be True to Form in Sudden Death

If your match goes to sudden death, you can expect the following from your opponent. The Bomber is going to try to end it quickly, so be prepared for him to make an early mistake. The Machine will try to drag it out until he bores you to death. You've got to try to take him out of his rhythm (more on this later in the chapter). The Magician is going to play you like a mouse, just looking for a crack so he can sneak in. Anytime you head to sudden death, it's almost impossible to call. Obviously, you and your opponent are evenly matched. Our suggestion: Try one of the sneaky tricks described below. They're all legal.

Gamesmanship: If It's Not Outside of the Rules, It's Not Cheating

Let's play a word-association game. Ready? Seve Balles . . . hey, we couldn't even get his name out before you hollered "Gamesmanship!" We can tell you watch a lot of golf on television. It's true, Seve Ballesteros *is* known as the king of gamesmanship, but there are two sides of the gamesmanship coin. Most sneaky tricks that are classified as gamesmanship are actually violations of accepted golf etiquette. If you look in your Rules book, you'll notice the very first section is on etiquette. You'll also notice there are no penalties for violations of etiquette. So whether or not you try any of the slick moves described below is up to you. Sometimes, if someone is really getting on your nerves, you can't help yourself—you just have to mess with his head. Or, in a really tight match, you might just be looking for any edge to push you over the top. If you want to try to get in your opponent's kitchen, we say have at it—you're not breaking any rules.

HOW TO TELL WHEN YOUR OPPONENT IS ABOUT TO CAVE IN TO THE PRESSURE

All players have patterns they fall into depending on the way they are playing. Knowing this can possibly allow you to detect a change in your opponent's performance during a match. Typically speaking, a downward slide is signaled by a change in preshot routine—a quicker than normal pace, with the player glancing over some elements and failing to spend enough time getting oriented to the target. Anytime a player starts hitting bad shots, you can be pretty sure that he's not performing his preshot routine in his normal manner (or that he has abandoned it completely). If you start to see some changes in your opponent's preshot routine, be ready to pounce. A few lousy shots on his part can't be far behind. Monitor his routine in the short game, too—his regular routine before a chip, pitch, or sand shot, and his normal routine before putting. If he's been stalking every putt like a caged lion for the first twelve holes, and suddenly just steps up and whacks one, you may be seeing a chink in the armor. As for your own game, if you start hitting some bad shots, double-check to make sure you're going through your routine at the same pace you do when you're playing well.

Here are a few more signs that your boy might be getting wobbly:

- His lips look very dry and he's licking them a lot.
- He continually looks at the ground between shots, or his shoulders are slumped. If he won't look at you, you definitely have him.
- He starts slamming clubs or displaying other signs of temper. Note: Don't confuse this with displays of temper early in the round. Those are typically performed by hotheads who need to blow off steam. A temper tantrum late in the round means your opponent is close to cracking.
- If it's not hot out and he continually wipes his brow, he's gagging. Same goes for sweating in general. If it's seventy degrees and he looks like he's in a sauna, he's feeling the heat in more ways than one.

It's good news for you whenever you start to see any of these signs. It means you don't have to do anything spectacular—just make a few pars and you'll be home free.

We'll leave you with these caveats before proceeding: One, if you decide to dish it out, expect to get it right back. Two, don't expect a handshake at the end of the round.

- **Planting the seed.** The idea behind this tactic is to plant a seed of doubt in your opponent while appearing to make friendly conversation. For example, you say, "This is a tough hole. There's out-of-bounds on the left." You may be able to break your opponent's concentration by forcing him to focus on this new bit of information. You must be careful, though, not to start worrying about that out-of-bounds yourself! Stay focused on your target and your swing keys, not consequences of the swing you're about to make. If you are focusing on getting the ball from point "A" to point "B," you won't be thinking of those negative things.
- **Taking him out of his rhythm.** This strategy can work brilliantly, especially if you're playing against a Machine! Try to establish your opponent's speed of play early, because it is possible to use that information to your advantage. The first rule of messing with someone's head by screwing up their pace is this: If you're playing against a player who plays at the same pace as you, then you should leave well enough alone and move on to some other tricks. There's no point in goading him to start possibly messing with you.

If you like to play fast, you're going to be a little uneasy at the beginning of most matches, since most everyday players have only two speeds: slow and slower. When you're up against a slower opponent, you have to try to force him into your rhythm, because if you don't, you're more susceptible to a blowup than any other type of player. The reason for this is that people who take their time on the golf course typically refuse to be rushed. In cases like this, you need to go to extreme measures to get the match on your pace. Here are a few tricks to make a slowpoke pick up the pace:

- If you're waiting for him to play on the tee and he's already hit, take off the second he hits his shot. If you're riding in a cart, be ready and take off. If you're walking, start walking right when he makes contact. Don't even wait for the ball to hit the ground.
- If you've hit to the green, start walking or driving to the green as soon as you put your club in the bag. Don't wait for him to play his approach shot, start making your way to the green. Don't take a path directly in front of him. Instead, stay off to the side where he won't see you while he's actually playing the shot, and keep moving while he does so. You'll be up at the green at about the same time as his ball, and he'll see you there.
- When you hole out, move immediately to the next tee box. If you've won the hole, play your tee shot as soon as you're ready to play—even if your opponent is still on the green behind you. Slow players love to dawdle on the greens hitting practice putts (which is legal in match play). This will help get them moving. You can bet anyone you play will be shocked to arrive at the tee to see you already down the fairway. Just remember not to play out of turn.
- Slow players get distracted more easily than quicker ones. So even if you can't speed them up, you might distract them as you walk out ahead if you get your clubs rattling together. Or if you have a noisy gas-powered cart!
- If your opponent is constantly gesturing to you to stop moving or to move to the side out of his view, just give him an innocent shrug and keep on moving. There's nothing in the Rules that says you can't move out ahead of the guy you're playing.

If you happen to be one of those slow players, you have less work to do than the fast player does. Basically, all you have to do is play your game and not let the above tactics get to you. When your opponent is walking out in front of you, simply wait until you're satisfied he's not going to distract you. The faster he goes, the more you should slow down. That will drive him nuts!

If you're neither overly slow nor super fast, you can try a mixture of these tactics. When you're playing the fast guy, just slow it down once in a while. Pretend you're going back to your bag to get a different club, even if you don't need one. Just take the one you have and put it back in the bag, then take it out again. Another trick to try is simply to linger over a few blades tossed in the air to check the wind. Do it two or three times for the same shot. Yet another move: Every so often go through your entire preshot routine, get set to play, then back off and do the entire thing again. This won't throw you off if you know you're going to do this before you go through the routine the first time. If you only mix these moves in once in a while, you might not get him pissed enough to have him start trying his tricks, and you might keep him off balance.

If you play at about-average speed and you're up against a slow player, you can mix in some of the pace-quickening techniques described above.

- **So tell me, Larry . . .** When you're standing around on the fourteenth or fifteenth tee casually chatting with everyone while you wait for the guys in the fairway to clear out, ask your opponent about his instructional history—especially if he's a Machine. He won't be able to resist. Just say something like, "So, have you been working with anyone on your game lately?" If you find out that he has taken a lesson within the last few weeks—especially the last few days— you've struck gold. Ask him what the pro taught him. If the teacher he worked with is like most pros, he probably tried to make a big swing change. If you find out that your opponent is working on a swing change, ask him to describe it to you—ask for all the details. For players in that position, it's almost inevitable that their game will fall apart during the round. Your inquiry may help it happen faster than normal. And as soon as he hits one bad shot, he'll be in that never-never land between his old swing and his new swing, and then you've got him. If you find yourself in this situation, take every chance you get to comment on his swing. Things like, "I can see what you're trying to do, Larry, and it looks like you're almost there."

- **Accuse him of a Rules violation.** In match play, the penalty for grounding the club in a hazard is loss of hole. While your opponent is walking into a bunker but before he plays a shot, say, "Hey, Joe, you didn't just drag your club on top of the sand, did you? Because that's against the Rules." After he stews about it for a few seconds, say, "Ah, don't worry about it. I was probably just seeing things."
- **The sealed lips routine.** If you notice your opponent likes to talk, you should clam up like a nun at a bachelor party. Don't say *anything*. Just shrug a lot, and don't smile. Don't even say, "Nice shot." On the other hand, if he's a quiet type, yammer away all day. Lee Trevino used to drive guys like Nicklaus crazy doing this.
- **Mark it, mister.** This is a great one. Ask the guy to mark his ball every single time it's your turn to putt—even if he's nowhere near your line.

If you're the type of guy who doesn't appreciate the artistry of gamesmanship, and someone tries pulling these stunts on you, just look up and say, "I assume you're not going to be pulling that crap all day." That usually works. Patiently wait for him to move well out of your range before you play any shot. Don't just sit there and stew about it because it will have an adverse effect on your game. On the other hand, the best way to get a guy who's trying to get you might just be not to let him know he's getting to you. Got it?

MASTERS OF MATCH PLAY: BEN HOGAN

Ben Hogan is one of only four players to win each of the four major professional championships at least once. He was the second player to do it (Gene Sarazen was the first), completing the task in 1953 when he won the British Open in his only appearance in that event. He might well have won the Grand Slam (all four majors in a single season) that year, but he had to settle for three because the British Open and the PGA Championship were played on conflicting dates.

Almost anyone who follows golf is aware of Hogan's courageous comeback from a near fatal accident when the car he was driving was hit by a bus—it is perhaps golf's most legendary tale. However, for the purposes of this book, we'll focus on another of Hogan's legacies: He was a monster in match play, going 22–5 in the PGA Championship and 3–0 in Ryder Cup play. In his only two trips to the PGA Championship finals (1946 and 1948), Hogan won 6 and 4, and 7 and 6.

What you can learn from Ben Hogan

As a match player, Hogan was merciless. After being crushed by Hogan 10 and 9 in the 1946 PGA Championship, Jimmy Demaret was asked if his friend Hogan had talked to him at all during the match. "Yeah," said Demaret, "he talked to me. The only thing he said all day was, 'You're away.' "

But of all the personal characteristics that appealed to the public about Hogan, the most appealing was that of Hogan the scientist—the experimenter who spent the majority of his waking hours thinking about, testing, and trying out, under the pressure of tournament play, the very best way to hit a golf ball. So it was not a surprise that one night while lying in bed, in the crystal-clear insight of half sleep, Hogan hit upon the secret of ball-flight control.

For ten years after he discovered his secret, Hogan remained stone silent as to its nature. Some of his fellow Tour pros doubted the merits of the Hawk's newly crafted fade ball flight. Max Faulkner, at the time the reigning British Open champion, once watched Hogan hitting practice balls and offered to help him "get rid of that fade." Hogan icily replied,

"You don't see the shag boy moving, do you?" Hogan revealed his three-part secret in an article in the August 8, 1955, issue of *Life,* after he had essentially retired from the Tour.

Pronation. When Scottish professionals came to this country in the late 1800s, they brought with them the idea of rolling the left hand and arm away from the ball in the backswing. This meant that the toe of the club fanned away faster than the heel of the club until, at the top of the backswing, both the back of the left hand and the palm of the right hand faced the sky. This idea was abandoned by most American tour players once steel shafts hit the scene, but Hogan recalled it in his early morning awakening and decided that this action set the club on its ideal swing plane. The problem was that the clubface was also pointed at the sky, in a closed position, at the top of the swing, promoting a hook. So, two additional changes were necessary.

The grip change. To gain more control of the club, Hogan moved his left thumb from a slightly strong position (left of the center of the shaft) to a completely neutral position, directly on top of the shaft. As a result, when he reached the top of his fully pronated backswing, his left thumb would be directly under the shaft, giving the club maximum stability and support.

The concave left wrist. The final portion of the secret was a slight bending of the left wrist toward the back of the head at the top of the backswing—roughly four to six degrees, just enough to produce wrinkles on that wrist. This movement rotated the clubface so that the toe of the club pointed at the ground at the top of the swing, no longer in a hook position. Hogan felt that by creating this antihook open position at the top of his backswing, he could swing as hard as he wanted because the club would never have enough time to get back to square (let alone closed) at impact.

With these changes, the fast-moving club approached the ball on a perfect plane and the clubface was slightly open at impact. The resulting powerful fade was easy to control—climbing to its apex, then sliding softly to the right as it floated to the ground. During the ten years of competition that Hogan used his secret, he won fifty tournaments, nine major titles, four PGA Player of the Year awards, and two money titles.

5.

Playing with a Partner

A few years back, PGA Tour player Ben Crenshaw was play-ing in a mixed-team event with some LPGA players. When Cren-shaw noted to Lanny Wadkins that he was hitting some shots from places he wasn't accustomed to playing, Wadkins cracked, "Yeah, like the fairway." That story emphasizes the plus side of playing with a partner, and since we most often play in groups of four, playing with a partner is something we do on a regular basis. To play a match against everyone in your group would be a little con-fusing. By playing with a partner, you have only one opponent in-stead of three. Playing with a partner is also a lot of fun since it gives you the feeling of being part of a team, and being on a team is part of the basic fabric of life—we do almost everything with other people. There is a downside to playing with a partner: You don't want to let him down. However, there are things you can do to improve your chances of success.

Picking a Partner

There are only two ways to end up with a partner in golf: You either pick one or one gets picked for you. Either way, you can make the partnership work by following the rules of a successful partnership that appear later in this chapter. The primary factor defining a good partnership is that it is made up of two different but compatible styles of play. In other words, the best partners are guys that play in a different style than you do. This gives you the best chance against the greatest variety of opponents. Same-style partnerships lack flexibility. It's sort of like driving down the center of the road—it only works if nothing unexpected happens. Here are how some partnerships tend to work:

- **Bomber and Machine:** A great pairing, it leaves the Bomber free to go wild while the Machine covers his ass when he gets in trouble.
- **Magician and Bomber:** Potentially, a devastating team. If they get on a roll, they will crush anyone they play.
- **Magician and Machine:** Not a super-potent combination, but could be the best on long, narrow courses. Depends on how the Magician drives the ball—bad (which might be okay) or *really* bad (which isn't okay).

It can be helpful if you know who you and your potential partner are going to be playing against. Here's how to counter if you know who you're playing:

- If you are a Machine and you're playing a partnership that features a Bomber, you might want to go with a Magician as your partner. The reason: The Bomber is always the dominant personality in any partnership, and that partnership will ride his emotional wave. The best way to keep the Bomber from getting fired up is to frustrate him by hanging with him even though he's outhitting you on the tee. The Bomber gets frustrated when *anyone* who can't hit as long as he does even manages to halve a hole with him. The Machine and Magician combo is one that will infuriate him, especially on a long, tight course, when he thinks his length should be an advantage, but where his lack of accuracy will kill him. Why not find another Bomber to counter the opposing Bomber? You could, but your Bomber partner might get into a slugging contest with the opposing Bomber and lose.

- If you're a Machine and the best player of the opposing partnership is a Magician, you should hook up with a Bomber. If you're lucky, the Bomber's bursts of spectacular play and your own steady play will be enough to win some holes when the Magician misses a few putts.
- If you're a Bomber and the dominant player on the opposition is a Machine, you should counter with a Magician. Nothing shuts down a Machine more effectively than losing the game of "golf swing." If the Machine thinks he's got a better swing and is a better player than both of you, he'll be homicidal when your partner starts getting up and down from the clubhouse roof.
- If you're a Bomber and the team you're facing is captained by a Magician, you can pair up with either a Magician of your own or a Machine. If you go with the Machine, remember they are susceptible to being frustrated by Magicians. A lot depends on the talent level of the Machine in question.
- If you're a Magician and you're up against a Big Bomber, you're already his nightmare opponent. So pick a Machine as your partner and you'll make his day even more miserable.
- If you're a Magician up against a great Machine, look for a Bomber as your partner. The Machine will practically be in tears before the day is over.

This book is about how to win at match play, so we assume you want to win every match you play. We realize that winning may not always be your greatest concern, but if it is, heed this advice: Stay away from picking your best buddy as your partner just because he's your best buddy, especially if his game is the same as your game (e.g., you're both Bombers). It helps to be friends with the person who is your partner, but close friendships can get in the way of winning. Sometimes you need to kick your partner in the ass and get him motivated, and your best pal may think you're just kidding or feel like you're taking an unnecessary shot at him.

The other thing about "best buddy" syndrome is that even if you *think* you don't care that much about winning, you *do* want to win. And if your boy starts tanking on you, things could get ugly.

We're not suggesting that you never play with your best friend as your partner. We're just saying that if you do, you have to tell yourself that you're just out for the fun and camaraderie and that you truly don't care whether you win or lose.

Of course, if your best buddy is Lanny Wadkins, you can ignore this advice.

There are some players you never, ever want as your partner if you can help it. So, since we're still talking about how to pick a partner, here are some things you should definitely avoid. They are perhaps obvious, but we want to make sure you've covered all the bases. So stay away from anyone who . . .

- Can't putt. How do you define "can't putt"? If he three putts more than twice in any given round, he can't putt.
- Is a known choker. Usually, the only way you can tell is if you've played with him before. If he makes less than half the realistically makable putts that "mean something" when you play with him, he's a choker. (A putt that "means something" is one to win or halve a hole.)
- Says something on the first tee such as, "All these bets are too confusing. You keep track and just tell me what I owe at the end." You should dump him faster than a mouthful of bees.

- Talks about every damned shot he hit after the round is over. Guys who yammer that much about their own games are usually trying to explain that they didn't play *that bad,* they just couldn't catch any breaks. The sign of a potentially good partner is that other people are always talking about how good he played.
- Depends on gamesmanship to win. On the other hand, a player who uses it sparingly, but effectively, may be first-rate partner material.
- Calls a lot of Rules violations, because he probably isn't focusing on outplaying the opponent.
- Complains he "can't believe that shot came up short/long." If he's too stupid to figure out the actual distance to the hole, he's too stupid to be your partner.
- Concedes putts that allow your opponent to win the hole. Or, even if you're both out of the hole, he concedes a birdie putt when birdies are worth points.
- Smashes a downhill putt fifteen feet past the hole and says (sincerely), "Boy, the greens are running fast today."

The Psychology of Playing with a Partner

As mentioned earlier, there are some downside risks associated with playing with a partner. Both players in a partnership must know what these risks are in order to avoid them.

Risk: You rely on each other too much. A partner is not a crutch you can use to cover your own bad play. You cannot depend on a partner to bail the team out every time you fall apart It's not a good idea to leave your partner alone against two other players. A good partner will occasionally cover your butt when you hit a bad shot—but the more bad shots you hit, the less likely he is to save you and your team.

Risk: *You try to force the action.* This is related to the previous problem. Sometimes when you have a lot of confidence in your partner, you are inclined to attempt shots that you aren't capable of making. Know the difference between shots you can pull off if you hit a perfect ball, and shots you cannot pull off if you have a perfect ball.

Risk: *You each worry about not letting the other down.* This is destructive and just adds to the pressure that you're already feeling. You and your partner should both realize that part of being partners is hanging tough through thick and thin. If you both acknowledge that bad shots are inevitable, and that you just have to play smart after you make one, no one is going to feel let down.

Risk: *You play outside your comfort zone.* Let's say you're a Bomber, and your partner hits a tee shot into trouble. Logic dictates that you play some sort of iron or fairway wood and get your ball in the fairway. Is this a smart move? It may be, but only once or twice a round. If you start playing to try to cover your partner's weaknesses on every hole, you'll be denying the team your strengths. Same would go if you were playing with a Bomber and he hit first and put his tee shot in the trees. If you're not a long hitter, you shouldn't step up and try to rip one because your big gun is in trouble. There are some strategies outlined a bit later on that can help you prevent some of these things from occurring.

Risk: *You suddenly feel like you can't think for yourself.* This happens quite frequently. A player gets in a team match and begins asking his partner everything: "Which way is the wind blowing, Lenny?" "Is it enough to make me take more club?" "How far is it to the green, Lenny?" "Where's the pin at?" "Which way is this going to break, Lenny?" You have to think for yourself.

Risk: *Your partner suddenly thinks you can't think for yourself.* What's more annoying than a partner who wants to ask your advice on every shot? A partner who wants to *give* advice before every shot. Here's the thing about advice: Unless the guy you're playing with is significantly better than you are and is more familiar with the course, he doesn't know any more about the game than you do. Now that we've told you not to take advice from your partner, here's our advice on that: If he insists on giving you some suggestion before every shot, find a new partner.

The Keys to a Successful Partnership

Beyond dissimilar but compatible styles of play, there are other things that go into making a partnership click. None of them are really big secrets, but something happens in the heat of competition that makes people forget them. So anytime a match is heating up, remember that all good match players are aware of what's going on around them. When you're playing with a partner, this means being aware of what's happening with him, too. These things will help turn your partnership into a dynamic duo.

The Rules of Winning with a Partner

1. Play your own game. There's an old saying in golf that goes something like this: "You've got to dance with the one you brought with you." This doesn't refer to your partner, but rather to your own game. As we've said before, you'll have your best chance for success if you stick with what you know.

2. Advice is asked for, not given. A good partner knows when to keep his mouth shut. Unless your partner is about to be attacked by a saber-toothed tiger, don't offer him advice. It will just muddle his thought process before playing a shot, particularly if your advice is the exact opposite of what he was thinking. Good partners will work this out before a match, especially as it relates to reading putts. Some players don't want their partners to read their putts, so don't do it for your partner unless he asks. When you do, remember you may have different styles of putting. For example, you may like to hit your putts firmly so they break less and your partner may like to hit them so they die at the hole, which means they are affected more by the break. You each may see the line a little differently.

3. When advice is asked for, it's given in measured amounts. You should administer advice to your partner as you would aspirin to a small child—just a little bit to ease any fears, but not enough to make matters worse. Partners should think of themselves as caddies. You want to give enough advice to help, but not enough to be blamed if things go wrong.

4. Administer advice as affirmation. When your partner asks for advice, don't just blurt out and answer. First, try to affirm whatever he's thinking as long as you think he's correct—or close to being correct. Do this by establishing what he's thinking. Here's an example of the wrong way of doing it.

Your partner: "Hey, Bob, what kind of yardage do you think I'm looking at here to carry the pond?"

You: "It's two hundred and one yards to the far side of that pond. You're out of your mind if you think you can carry that."

Now, here's an example of a more successful communication between partners.

Your partner: "Hey, Bob, what kind of yardage do you think I'm looking at here to carry the pond?"

You: "What are you thinking, Zeus?"

Your partner: "I reckon it's about one hundred and ninety to the far side."

You: "That sounds about right. I think it might be a few more than that, maybe two hundred. Make sure you hit a shot you're comfortable with."

When your partner asks your advice, he's not looking for details. He's trying to make sure his own thoughts were in the ballpark of being correct. This holds true when you ask for advice. You should know your own game well enough that you already have a pretty good idea of what you want to do and use your partner's feedback as affirmation.

5. High-risk shots are briefly discussed. When either member of a partnership is going to attempt a shot with a high-risk-and-reward value, he should let the other guy know before he does it. Ultimately, the decision is up to the one attempting the shot, but at least give the other guy a chance to formulate an alternative strategy. This gives you both a chance to say something simple like, "Okay. You've got to hit it perfect. Go for it." This will cause a brief reexamination of the risk, just to make sure the shot is realistic.

6. One partner never assumes he knows what the other one is thinking. If it's your turn to play and you really want to know what your partner plans on doing with his next shot, ask him. If he ends up doing something other than what you expected, you're going to end up thinking or saying, "I thought you were going to play for the center of the green. I didn't know you were going to gun right at it (and subsequently hit it in the water)."

7. There are no expectations. You want your partner to play well, but you shouldn't expect him to. Before the round starts, the two of you should make a deal: no saying "Sorry" after a blown putt or chunking wedge into the water. Just move on to the next hole and play.

The Strategy of Playing with a Partner

Who Should Play First from the Tee?

In four-ball. Partners can juggle their order of play as much as they like in a four-ball. Off the tee, it depends on the makeup of the team and the hole.

MASTERS OF MATCH PLAY: TOM WATSON

The record book doesn't tell you everything you need to know about Tom Watson, but it does tell an unmistakably impressive story. Watson won five British Open titles, just one shy of the total won by long-ago great Harry Vardon. He also won two Masters championships (where he also holds a record for twenty-one consecutive cuts made) and one U.S. Open. Those numbers don't even hint at how Watson dominated the PGA Tour from 1974 to 1984. During those years he was never lower than twelfth on the money list, and topped the list five times. He was the PGA Player of the Year six times during that same stretch, and he won three consecutive Vardon Trophies for lowest scoring average on tour. But as we said, the numbers don't tell Watson's story in full.

What you can learn from Tom Watson

The biggest thing you can learn from Tom Watson cannot be learned on the lesson tee, and that is fearlessness. You have to develop that quality from within. (Although it does help your fearless factor if you practice hard and improve your game. The better you are the less afraid you are to win.) Even though Watson's well-remembered triumphs over Nicklaus were at stroke play, he applied that same fearlessness at match play, compiling a 10-4-1 record in four Ryder Cup appearances. Watson was only 2–2 in singles competition, but in partnership with Nicklaus and others, he was Tom Terrific. In 1983, Watson went 3–1 in partner play with *three different* partners. (He even managed to help Ben Crenshaw win a point!) In all, Watson played with seven different partners in Ryder Cup play—a clear signal that he was a player capable of making a great partner to any player.

His winning mind-set aside, Watson's game at its peak was defined by several things: imaginative shots, great scrambling ability, deft putting, and splendid tempo. The first three things made him a perfect partner. The last—tempo—is something you can use in your own game even when you're just practicing or playing a match.

The word *tempo* is probably one of the most misunderstood words in golf. Most everyday golfers confuse tempo with swinging slowly, when in fact tempo means to swing the club *at the same pace* throughout your swing. This is an important distinction, because some people can't do anything slowly, and if they think they have to swing the golf club slowly it screws up their games. That's exactly why Watson is still a good example of what tempo means. Watson doesn't do anything slowly in his golf game: He thinks quickly, walks quickly, sets up quickly, and makes quick, crisp strikes at the ball. The key is he does it all at the same pace—he doesn't have one of those tension-creating moments in his swing when he attempts to speed the club up or slow it down. It's moving fast the entire time. The way to set your own personal tempo is to adapt the pace of your everyday life into your golf game. If you like to do things quickly, copy Tom Watson. If you like to do things slowly, copy someone like Fred Couples. As long as you keep the pace—the tempo—consistent throughout your swing, you won't have any problems.

Long or medium-length hole. *Bomber and Machine:* The Bomber is at his best when he's freewheeling. The Machine should hit first and put the ball in play. This also helps alleviate some pressure on the Machine, since if he hits first he doesn't know for a fact that his partner is out of play yet—there is still hope. An exception: Late in the match on narrow driving holes, let the Bomber go first. It doesn't play to his strength either way, but if he gets the first blast in and it goes straight, it puts some major heat on the opposition. *Bomber and Magician:* Let the Bomber go first. Since the Magician doesn't care where his own ball goes as long as it's not out of bounds, this gives the Bomber a free pass. *Machine and Magician:* The Machine. It will let him proceed in an orderly way, and he won't have to react immediately when the Magician carves one into the trees.

Par three. *Bomber and Machine:* The Machine should go first. Nothing he does is going to affect the Bomber, but an implosion by the Bomber may rattle the Machine. *Bomber and Magician:* Let the Magician go first. They eat up par threes, and even if he misses the green, the Bomber can feel confident that the Magician is still in the hole. *Machine and Magician:* Again, the partner should have confidence in the Magician and let him go first. If he hits a good one, it takes some pressure off the Machine. If he hits a stinker, it doesn't apply any more pressure on the Machine.

In foursomes. The only decision to make here is who is going to lead off and close out the match for you on the tee. Who closes it out is probably more important. It might help if you know the course and it just happens to run roughly in an order that favors your team's combination, i.e., you're a terrific Magician and all the par threes are even-numbered holes. It's unlikely, but worth a check. Normally though, you'll want to think about who will be hitting the tee shot on the final hole should the match reach that point. Your options:

The eighteenth is a narrow driving hole. *Bomber and Machine:* You want the Bomber to go first on the last hole, even if it's narrow. The logic: The Bomber is the only player capable of deciding a hole with a tee shot. A long straight one—if he can pull it off— can be intimidating, and force second-shot mistakes for the opposition before the Machine has to play his second shot. If they've tanked by then, he'll be riding high. The Machine has to trust his strengths in this position. So, the Machine should play the tee shot on the first hole. *Bomber and Magician:* Same as above, since even if the Bomber hits a wild tee shot at eighteen, the Magician can bail the team out. *Machine and Magician:* Let the Machine go first at eighteen (and second at the first hole), unless the Magician is a hybrid Bomber/Magician. Then let the Machine lead off at the first and the Bomber/Magician take a rip at it on the eighteenth tee.

The eighteenth is wide open from the tee. *Bomber and Machine:* Let the Bomber take you out on the first hole. If he's loose and ready, a cannon shot from the first tee could set the tone for the entire day against a weaker opponent. *Bomber and Magician:* Same thing—give the Bomber the rock on the first tee. *Machine and Magician:* Let the Machine take you out on the first. The Magician is most unpredictable at the beginning of the match. By the time you reach the eighteenth tee, he'll have found his swing (if he's going to find it on a given day).

Who Should Play First on the Approach?

First, a clarification on the question. The Rules allow the players in a partnership to play in whatever order they like as long as it's the team's turn to play. (The Rule, number 30-3c, reads: "Balls belonging to the same side may be played in the order the side considers best.") In other words, as long as one of you is away, either one of you can play. Generally speaking, your best bet is to proceed as usual once play has begun on a hole, except in the following scenarios.

One ball is much longer off the tee than the other, but may be in trouble. In this situation, the long-ball hitter has to hustle himself up to where his ball is and make a determination. He should tell his partner one of these things: (a) "I've got a clear swing and a clear shot. Play your normal shot"; (b) "I have a shot, but it's a risky one. I can either play the risky shot now and you can play a shot knowing that I'm in or out of the hole, or you can go ahead and play and I'll just wait and see"; or (c) "I'm dead and I'll have to take a drop. Play hard, pard." The key is to leave the decision in the hands of the player who is away.

Both players face major risk-and-reward approaches. In this situation, there is only one way to proceed. You should decide which of you is more likely to pull the shot off (making certain to consider all the variables) and let that player go first. The logic: If he makes it, you can still go for it and maybe get two balls in close. If he misses, you can play it safe, but at least there was a chance you were going to get two shots at it. If you lay up first and he goes for it and fails, your team only has one chance at a good score instead of two.

Who Should Putt First?

Things can get confusing on the greens and you have to assess each situation as it arises. The best rule is to leave any decisions up to the player whose turn it is to putt. The possible scenarios are endless: Players lagging up close to the hole so their partner has a "free" run at a winning putt; players putting to show their partner the line or the speed of a putt near the hole; the list goes on and on. There are no rules here. You just have to weigh each situation and the personalities involved when the moment arrives. Actually, there is one rule: Don't try and force what you think on your partner. Don't *tell* him you're going to do anything. If you want to suggest something, say, "I'm sure you know we have some options here, Duke. You just let me know if you need me to help out."

GREAT MOMENTS IN THE RYDER CUP: SEVE BALLESTEROS AND JOSE MARIA OLAZABAL— THE SPANISH ARMADA

The Ryder Cup is a treat for golf fans for many reasons, one of them being that they get to see the world's best players play as partners in match play. A good many of the matches everyday golfers play are with a partner— it's one of the most fun things a golfer can do. In the history of partnerships, none was ever more successful than the Ryder Cup pairing of Spaniards Seve Ballesteros and Jose Maria Olazabal. Ballesteros was 20-12-5 as a Ryder Cup competitor, and through 1997 Olazabal was 14-8-3. Theirs was the perfect partnership—they fueled each other to new heights, Olazabal feeding off the energy of the older Ballesteros, and Seve reveling in the feeling of mentoring Olazabal.

Ballesteros cut his teeth in the Ryder Cup the hard way, losing four of a possible five points in the 1979 competition, the first to include players from continental Europe. In his first four matches, he and countryman Antonio Garrido encountered the best learning experience rookie Ryder Cuppers could want: three matches against Lanny Wadkins and Larry Nelson, two of the toughest competitors of all time. (Wadkins's match-play skill is legendary, but people often overlook the quietly fierce Nelson, who was 9-3-1 lifetime in the Cup.) The Spaniards lost all three matches, and Ballesteros lost to Nelson 3 and 2 in the singles competition. Steel is made from fire, however, and when Ballesteros next appeared in the Ryder Cup, he won three points for his side.

By the time the 1987 Ryder Cup rolled around, Captain Jacklin had hit upon an idea. The youngest member on his squad was the talented but inexperienced Olazabal. Jacklin thought the rookie and the now veteran Ballesteros (by this time a multiple winner of the Masters and the British Open) might click. Jacklin's hunch was correct—the pairing won three of four matches. When it came time for the 1989 edition of the Cup, Jacklin called on the two again, and they came through again, with three victories and one halve. The Spanish Armada was born.

In the tussle at Kiawah Island in 1991, the Armada took off again, this time winning three more and halving another. Together, Ballesteros and Olazabal seemed invincible: In their first twelve matches together they were 9-1-2! Things reached a stage where it seemed the Europeans could count on a point every time the two went out. In the first morning match at The Belfry in 1993, the Armada sputtered, losing to Tom Kite and Davis Love III. The Spaniards rebounded to crush the same American pairing 4 and 3 that afternoon. The next morning, they beat Kite and Love again, raising their record to an incredible 11-2-2. And just like that, the run ended. Seve was tired, and Captain Bernard Gallacher decided to rest him that afternoon. Olazabal went out with Swede Joakim Haeegman, and lost 2 and 1 to Raymond Floyd and Payne Stewart. For the 1995 Ryder Cup at Oak Hill, the Armada couldn't even make it out of dry dock. Just one year after winning the Masters, Olazabal was out of action with a foot injury. When he returned to the Cup in 1997, Seve was gone from the competition, serving as the captain for Europe's 14½ to 13½ victory.

6.

The Rules of Match Play

You could devote the remainder of your life to understanding the Rules of Golf and still not quite get them. Even at the U.S. Open, which is run by the United States Golf Association (USGA), there are sometimes Rules mishaps, and the USGA writes the Rules. The first rule about the Rules is that you should always carry a copy in your bag if you want to be a serious match player. If you don't have a copy, you can get one by calling the USGA at (908) 234-2300, or by visiting their Web site at www.usga.org.

The Rules for stroke play and the Rules for match play are the same for the most part. There are some differences in the actual Rules, but mostly it's a matter of different penalties for violations of a Rule. We've selected the Rules that are the most commonly violated by everyday players, and thus the ones that create uneasy situations where you might have to confront an opponent. (This doesn't happen in stroke play, since you don't have an opponent.) We've also selected some definitions on procedures, such as how to drop when a ball goes in the water, so you can avoid any attempts by your opponent to circumvent the Rules.

To have any clue about how to interpret the Rules, you must first understand some definitions. So we organized this chapter by giving you a definition of something, giving you the main gist of the Rule, and offering some examples. However, the most important Rule to remember in serious competition is that you and your opponent cannot agree to waive any Rule. If you do, you're both disqualified.

Advice: Advice is any counsel or suggestion that could influence a player in determining his play, the choice of a club, or the method of making a stroke. Information on the Rules or on matters of public information, such as the position of hazards or the flagstick on a putting green, is not advice. The Rule on advice (8-1) reads as follows: "During a stipulated round, a player shall not give advice to anyone in the competition, except his partner. A player may ask for advice during a stipulated round only from his partner or either of their caddies." If you violate this rule, you lose the hole.

Here's how this Rule works:

- It's okay for you to look in your opponent's bag to see what club he is hitting. If he puts a towel over the clubs, you can move the towel. You just can't *ask* for advice. It's also okay for you to ask him where the flagstick is on a given hole, or the distance or par of a hole, or what he's going to have for dinner that night.
- You have to be wary of inadvertently breaking this Rule. Sometimes you just instinctively blurt out, "Great shot. What club did you hit?" That's a penalty, even if you didn't mean to ask. If you ask and your opponent answers, there is no penalty on him.
- If your opponent has a caddie, you can't ask his caddie what club he hit or what club he thinks you should hit. The bad guys can't ask your caddie, either.

- You can't "accidentally" spout out incorrect advice. Here's an example: You hit a shot and say, "I haven't hit a five-iron flush all day." But it wasn't actually a five-iron, it was a six-iron. Maybe, you claim, you were just talking to yourself, and besides, it's not advice because it was incorrect. Doesn't matter—the Rule doesn't distinguish between good advice and bad advice.

Ball in play: A ball is in play as soon as the player has made a stroke on the teeing ground. It remains in play until it is holed out, lost, out of bounds, lifted, or another ball has been substituted, whether or not the Rules permitted that substitution. The idea of a ball in play pops up in a number of places, but the really interesting notions involve the ball moving unexpectedly or hitting something.

Rule 18 is all about a ball in play, but at rest, which suddenly moves or is moved. Under the Rule, "moved" means the ball left its position and came to rest elsewhere. If it does move, there is often no penalty and other times only a stroke. Unless you decide to kick it out from behind a tree—then you lose the hole.

The first condition covered is when the ball is moved by an "outside agency." (An outside agency is anything that's not part of the match. You, your partner, opponents, caddies, and equipment are *not* outside agencies. A dog who runs onto the green and picks up your ball is an outside agency. In *Caddyshack,* when Rodney Dangerfield's ball gets stuck on that bird's beak, the bird is an outside agency.) If your ball is at rest and it is moved by an outside agency, there is no penalty as long as you replace the ball before you make your next stroke. *Wind and water are not outside agencies.*

If your ball is in play and you, your partner, or either of your caddies lifts it, moves it, *purposely* touches it, or causes it to move (except as permitted by other Rules), it's a one-stroke penalty. If your equipment or your partner's equipment causes your ball to move, it's a one-stroke penalty. The following are times when you're *not* penalized for your ball moving: if you accidentally move it while measuring to see which ball is farthest from the hole; while searching for it in a hazard, ground under repair, or casual water; if you give it a little nudge while fixing a ball mark or hole plug; if you're brushing loose impediments from the green and you brush the ball, too; if you're lifting a ball under a Rule; if you cause it to move while removing a movable obstruction.

But this Rule can get you when you least expect it. If a player's ball in play moves after he has addressed it, the player is deemed to have moved the ball and incurs a penalty stroke. The player should replace the ball, unless it moves after his swing and he does not stop his swing. So when exactly have you addressed the ball? Once you've taken your stance *and* grounded the club behind the ball. (You cannot ground your club in a hazard, but when you're in one you've addressed the ball once you've taken your stance.) Perhaps you've noticed that Jack Nicklaus never grounds his clubs—not even his putter—behind the ball. This is because if you do, and the ball moves, it costs you a stroke. This is most important on the greens, especially when you remember that wind *is not* an outside agency. So on windy days, be careful on the greens.

If you're brushing loose impediments on the green and you bump your ball, that's okay—you just put the ball or your marker back where it was. But if you're moving loose impediments within one club-length of your ball through the green, and your ball moves even before you've addressed it, that's a one-shot penalty. (Through the green is the entire course except the tee and green on the hole you're playing and hazards.) Same goes for your partner or caddie moving stuff around your ball. If this happens, replace the ball.

Every so often you'll be looking for a ball in the trees or leaves and someone helping you look will kick it. If anyone other than you kicks your ball or steps on it, there's no penalty—you just put it back. If you kick it, and you're not in a hazard, that costs you a penalty stroke. If you're not searching for your ball and your opponent or his caddie or his equipment moves your ball, that's a one-shot penalty on your opponent, and you replace the ball.

If another ball hits your ball at rest and sends it flying, there's no penalty on anyone. Just put the ball back.

All of the above concerns your ball when it is in play and at rest. What about when your ball is in motion—in midflight? That's a different story. If you play a shot and it hits you, your partner, your caddies, or equipment, you lose the hole. Doesn't matter if the ball comes to a full stop or is deflected—you still lose the hole. If your ball hits any of your opponents or their stuff, you have two options. You can play the ball as it lies after it comes to rest, or you can go back to the original spot and play the shot over, no penalty. If you hit the ball inside an opponent's bag or cart or sweatshirt, you can drop the ball where the article was when the ball came to rest in it. If it was on the green, you don't have to drop it, you can place it.

Bunker: A bunker is a hazard consisting of a prepared area of ground, often a hollow, from which turf or soil has been removed and replaced with sand. Grass-covered ground bordering, and around, the bunker is not part of the bunker. A ball is considered in a bunker when it lies in or touches any part of the sand.

When your ball is in a bunker, you cannot ground your club before playing a shot. If you do, you lose the hole. You can't test the condition of the sand by scooping up a handful, either. Now, if you trip and you're about to fall on your face, you can use your club to prevent you from falling. If you're in a bunker and fail to escape, you can rake the sand at the first spot before playing the next shot as long as you don't improve the lie of the ball. You cannot touch loose impediments in a bunker. If you do, you lose the hole. However, if you can't see your ball and there's a pile of flower buds in the bunker, you can, without penalty, brush enough of the loose impediments away to determine that a ball is there. If you accidentally move more stuff than needed, just put it back on the ball, no penalty. You're only really trying to see a part of the ball. You're not entitled to see the entire thing, nor do you need to, because there is no penalty for playing a wrong ball from a hazard.

Casual water: Casual water is any temporary accumulation of water on the course that is visible before or after you take your stance. That's as long as you're not in a water hazard, Einstein. A ball is in casual water when it lies in or touches any part of the casual water. You're entitled to a drop if the casual water affects your stance or your line of intended swing, or when the ball is just sitting in it. The good thing to know here is that even if you have a good lie but you're standing in casual water, you can still lift the ball and drop it clear of the casual water. It's a good idea to do so. It'll give you better footing.

Equipment: Equipment is anything used, worn, or carried by or for the player. The important thing to know is that this includes golf carts, whether motorized or not. If the cart is being shared, it is considered the equipment of the person whose ball is involved in a Rules situation. An exception: If the cart is actually moving and the other person sharing it is moving it, then the cart is considered his equipment.

The equipment Rules are fairly easy to remember, and they can come in handy if you're playing against someone who likes to throw clubs, so listen up.

If the playing characteristics of a club are changed during a round because of damage sustained in the normal course of play, you can use the club in its altered state, or, without unduly delaying play, repair it. Note that this says in the *normal* course of play. Smashing a club on the ground, or against a tree or golf cart, is not the normal course of play. If you bend a club in anger or otherwise maim it, you cannot use it during the rest of the round. So if you're playing against some fool who smashes his putter against a tree and bends the shaft, then uses it to putt on the next green, call him on it. He is disqualified, and you win on the spot.

The same is true if you catch someone with grease on the club or the ball, an old trick that reduces the spin on the ball. That's a disqualification also.

Amazingly, some players act as if there is no Rule regarding the number of clubs that are allowed to be carried during competition. The maximum number of clubs you can carry is fourteen. If you start out with *less* than fourteen clubs, you can add up to fourteen while you're playing, as long as you don't hold up play. This would mean sending a caddie to get the other club(s), or waiting until you make the turn. If you damage a club in the normal course of play, you can also replace it, provided you don't hold up play. You cannot borrow clubs from other players on the course, not even your partner. However, you and your partner can share clubs if the total between the two of you is no more than fourteen. This is only practical if neither one of you has a full set.

If during your match you discover you or your opponent has more than fourteen clubs in the bag, the match is adjusted by deducting one hole for each of the holes where the breach occurred. It doesn't matter if they are holes won or halved, they are automatic losses for the Rule violator. There's a two-hole limit on the penalty, however, so if you catch him (or yourself) at the second hole or beyond, you still only get two holes deducted from the score.

Once it is determined the number of clubs is greater than fourteen, enough clubs must be declared out of play until the number in play is only fourteen. If any of the clubs declared out of play is subsequently used to play a stroke, the offender is disqualified. End of match.

Ground under repair: Ground under repair is any portion of the course so marked by order of the Committee. (The Committee is the Rules Committee if there is one for a competition. If there is no competition, it's the Greens Committee. If you're playing at a

public course, ask the pro or the greenkeeper.) Ground under repair includes material piled for removal and a hole made by a
greenkeeper, even if it's not marked as ground under repair.
Ground under repair is usually marked with white paint, sometimes stakes. The markings are considered part of the ground under repair. If the markings are stakes, the stakes are considered
obstructions.

Hazard: A hazard is any bunker or water hazard.

Holed: A ball is holed when it is at rest within the circumference
of the hole *and* all of it is below the level of the lip of the hole.

If your ball is resting against the flagstick and not completely beneath the level of the lip, you or your partner or caddie (if you tell
him to) can move or remove the flagstick so the entire ball falls below the level of the lip. If the ball cooperates, you're deemed to have
holed out with your last stroke. We recommend just pulling the
stick to one side rather than yanking it out. If you yank it out and
the ball comes with it, you have to place the ball next to the hole
and tap it in. There's no penalty, but it costs you an extra stroke.

Honor: The side entitled to play from the teeing ground is said to
have the honor.

Lateral water hazard and water hazard: A lateral water hazard
is a water hazard, or part of one, so situated that you cannot drop a
ball "behind" it in accordance with Rule 26-1b. (That's the regular water hazard rule.) A lateral hazard should be defined by red
stakes or red painted lines on the ground. A ball is in the hazard
when it lies on or touches any part of the line. A water hazard is
any water that isn't a lateral water hazard. Water hazards should be
marked by yellow lines or stakes. Those stakes and lines are part of
the hazard, so if any part of your ball touches them, you're in the
hazard. The stakes are obstructions.

The first thing you have to do when your ball heads toward a water hazard is make certain it did indeed go in the hazard. Here's a direct quote from the Rules: "It is a question of fact whether a ball lost after having been struck toward a water hazard is lost inside or outside the hazard. In order to treat the ball as lost in a hazard, there must be reasonable evidence that the ball lodged in it. In the absence of such evidence, the ball must be treated as a lost ball."

Once you've established that the ball did go into the hazard, you may proceed as follows, under penalty of one stroke. But don't forget, you have to count the stroke you played the ball with, too, so in effect it's a two-stroke goof-up.

- You can play another ball from the spot the original ball was played.
- You can drop a ball behind the water hazard, keeping the point at which the ball last crossed the margin of the water hazard directly between the hole and the spot where the ball is dropped, with no limit to how far back you go from the hazard.
- If it's a lateral water hazard, you have two other options. You can drop a ball outside the hazard and two club lengths (no nearer the hole) from the point the ball crossed the hazard line. Or you can drop a ball on the opposite side of the lateral water hazard, equidistant from the hole.

Under any of the above options, you can lift and clean the ball. There are no exceptions to these procedures, so watch your opponent carefully when he hits a ball in the water.

Line of play and area of swing: The line of play is the direction you wish the ball to take after a stroke, plus a reasonable distance on either side of that line. The line of play goes to, but not beyond, the hole. The area of intended swing is the path you think the club is going to move along.

You cannot improve your line of play or area of intended swing by doing any of the following:

- Moving, bending, or breaking anything growing or fixed, including immovable obstructions and objects defining out of bounds.
- Removing or pressing down sand, loose soil, replaced divots, other cut turf placed in position, or other irregularities of the surface.

Line of putt: The line you expect a putt to take, with a reasonable amount of room on either side. Rule 16-1e forbids a player from making a putt while his stance is astride or his feet touch the line of the putt. The penalty is loss of hole.

Loose impediments: Loose impediments are natural objects such as leaves, twigs, branches, and other stuff from trees or dung, worms, insects and casts or heaps made by them, provided they are not fixed or growing, are not solidly embedded, and do not adhere to the ball. You can move them, just don't move the ball.

On the green, sand and loose soil are considered loose impediments. They are not loose impediments anywhere else.

Snow and natural ice are casual water or loose impediments, so it's up to you how to proceed. If you decide they are loose impediments, you can move them. If you decide they are casual water, you can take a drop without penalty. Neither frost nor dew is a loose impediment or casual water—it's just frost—so deal with it and hit the shot. Manufactured ice, like the kind some clod would dump out of his cooler, is a movable obstruction, so move it.

Lost ball: A ball is lost if it is not found within five minutes of the time when the search began for it by you, your partner, and your caddies if you have any. If you put another ball into play, under the Rules the original ball is lost, even if you haven't searched for it. The ball is also lost if you play a stroke with a provisional ball from the place where the original ball is likely to be or from a point nearer the hole than that place. (See *provisional ball*.)

If you lose a ball and you didn't play a provisional, you have to march back to the spot you originally played from and play again. You add a penalty stroke and the original stroke to your score. So if you lost your tee shot, for example, you'd be playing your third stroke from the tee. If this happens to your opponent, don't settle for the old line, "Oh, I'll just drop here and take a stroke." That's not how it's done, and he's not incurring the distance part of the penalty.

Obstruction: An obstruction is anything artificial, including the surfaces and sides of roads and paths and manufactured ice. (They go to great lengths in the Rules to reduce the number of manufactured ice incidents!) These things are not obstructions: anything used to denote out of bounds such as walls, fences, stakes, railings, etc.; any part of an immovable artificial object that is out of bounds; any construction deemed to be an integral part of the course. (That would be a bridge or something like that.) *Artificial* in this Rule doesn't mean it has to be manufactured, it just means it wasn't intended to be part of the course. A tree limb lying on the ground would be an obstruction.

If the obstruction is easily moved, it is classified as a movable obstruction. If the ball does not lie on or in the obstruction, you can move the thing. If the ball moves, just replace it. If the ball is on top of something or inside of something, you may lift the ball without penalty, move the object, and drop the ball if you're not on the green. If you're on the green, you can place the ball.

If the obstruction can't be moved, under the Rules it's an immovable obstruction. If it interferes with your stance or area of intended swing you can lift and drop at the nearest point on the course that frees you from interference by the obstruction. You cannot cross the obstruction, go through it or under it, and you cannot move nearer to the hole. You cannot drop in a hazard or on the green, either. When you do drop, you must do so within one club length of the spot of the point that fulfills all the above criteria. Unless you're on the putting green, it doesn't matter if the obstruction blocks your line of play. And you don't find too many immovable obstructions on the greens. You can read this to mean that you're not entitled to give yourself a clear shot—only a clean stance and swing.

Out of bounds: This is ground from which you cannot play. It's defined by white reference stakes or a fence or a wall. The score-card will usually tell you which holes have out of bounds. (Read the back of it.) If the out of bounds is defined by a line painted on the ground, the line itself is out of bounds. When the boundary is marked by stakes, you use the *inside* part of the stakes for reference—that's the part closest to the course. If the stakes have angled supports holding them up, they don't figure into the boundary marking. A ball is only out of bounds when *all of it is out of bounds.* You can stand out of bounds and play a ball that is in bounds. (Whew, that was a close one.) When a ball is hit out of bounds, there is only one course of action: Another ball must be played from the original spot. The fine is one penalty plus the original stroke, so on the replay the third stroke is being played.

Partner: A partner is a player on the same side as you are. In a threesome, foursome, or four-ball match, when the Rules say "player," this includes your partner or partners. Speaking of partners, if you and your partner get screwed up in a foursome match and play out of sequence, you lose the hole.

Provisional ball: A provisional ball is a ball played under Rule 27-2, when your original ball *may* be lost (not including in a water hazard) or may be out of bounds. If you're going to play a provisional ball, you must declare it as such to your opponent. If you don't, that ball is automatically in play. Once you proceed to play a second shot with the provisional ball, your opponents are going to assume you've put that ball in play and that the original is lost. In most cases this is true, unless you badly mis-hit the provisional and it's one hundred yards or so short of the whereabouts of the original ball. Under these conditions, you *can* play a second shot with the provisional without putting it in play, but you'd better clear it first with your opponent. If the provisional does eventually end up in play, you obviously must count all strokes played with it.

Putting green: A ball is on the putting green when any part of it touches the putting green. The fringe is not the putting green.

If you play a shot from the putting green and you hit another ball on the green, there's no penalty. (This is unique to match play. In stroke play, if you putt on the green and hit another ball on the green, that's a big two-shot fine.) Now, if you're on the green and you putt while another ball is still in motion, it gets a little delicate. If you were away and someone else played out of turn, you're safe—no penalty. If you weren't away, and another player's ball is still moving when you putt, you lose the hole. And if two balls in motion collide on the green after being played from the green, whoever wasn't away loses the hole.

In any type of golf, the player who is farthest from the hole ("away") always has the right to play. So, if you are playing a match and your ball is on your opponent's line and he asks you to mark it, do so. If you decide you're going to outsmart him and putt it rather than mark it, he can force you to replay the stroke—which he's definitely going to do if you make the putt. (And you never want to have to make *any* putt twice.) If you miss, he probably won't care.

Here's another situation: You're playing a match and you hit a putt that is hanging right on the edge of the hole, looking as if it may topple in. Your opponent quickly moves up and knocks it away (which is an acceptable way of conceding a putt). He says, "That's good," and you think, "That's bulls—t." And you're right. The Rules say that you have to move into position to play the next putt without delay, but once doing so have ten seconds to wait to see if the ball drops in. If your opponent knocks it away before those ten seconds are up, you win the hole.

Here's a twist on that one: Let's say it's a beautiful sunny day and you hit a putt that's hanging on the lip. You get up to the ball and during your ten-second wait you intentionally decide to position your body so your shadow is over the ball. What you're hoping is that the shadow will cool the grass and it will bend, toppling the ball into the hole. Sure enough, it happens—the ball goes in. Next thing you know your opponent is jumping up and down screaming, "One dash two! You violated Rule one dash two, you cheating SOB!" What he means is you exerted undue influence on the ball. According to the strict interpretation of the Rule, he's wrong and what you did was just plain smart. Good move.

Depending on the type of courses you play, here's a little-known Rules violation that can work in your favor. Let's say you're tending the flagstick as your opponent putts, and as you pull the flag out, the hole liner comes with it. If this ever happens to you, don't yank it all the way out! If you get it stuck halfway and the ball hits the liner and stops, the guy putting is out of luck. If the cup liner is stationary when the ball hits it, he has to place the ball on the edge of the hole and tap in the next putt (after you replace the liner). If the cup liner is actually moving when the ball hits it, he has to replay the putt. Either way, there is no penalty and you get a good laugh at his expense.

(Here's a real crafty move to try if you feel like getting nasty: If you're on the green and your opponent asks you to tend the flag, just say, "No." You're not bound to tend the flag by the Rules.)

Here's a situation that occurs more often than you might realize: Your opponent has a long putt and asks you to tend the flag. He hits the putt and as the ball gets to the hole you fail to remove the stick and his ball hits it. What happens? Any one of these three things: (1) If you did it on purpose, in other words, you were trying to get him to incur a penalty by hitting the flagstick, then you are disqualified. That's it, pack your bags, you're out! (2) If you left the flag in out of the goodness of your heart because the guy hammered the putt and you didn't want the ball to roll off the green, you're just plain stupid. You lose the hole. (3) If you failed to pull the flagstick because you just weren't paying attention or it got stuck, or you closed your eyes or got so excited you forgot what was going on, there is no penalty on you but there is on the other poor fool. He loses the hole. In these situations, other than a fistfight, the only way to decide what the hell happened is to defer to the Committee.

Rule 16-1e provides you with a great way to nail someone, because the line of the putt extends back through the ball. This Rule gets broken all the time when guys are tapping putts into the hole. If they stand on a straight line going from the hole through the ball and to the end of the continent on which you're playing, they've violated 16-1e. Watch 'em close when they move in for the tap-ins. Penalty: Loss of hole.

Side: A side is a player or two or more players who are partners.

Stance: You've taken your stance when you've put your feet in position preparatory to playing a stroke. You are entitled to place your feet firmly while taking your stance, but you cannot "build" a stance. This means you cannot place anything under your feet for support (or a towel under your knees if you're hitting a ball from under a tree). If you do, you lose the hole.

Stroke: A stroke is the forward movement of the club made with the intention of fairly striking at and moving the ball. If you check your downswing voluntarily before the clubhead reaches the ball, that is not a stroke. (Note it says "reaches" the ball, not strikes the ball. So if you whiff, that counts as a stroke, even if you don't hit the ball.)

A concession of a stroke or of a hole or of a match cannot be declined and it cannot be withdrawn. Once you've conceded, it's a done deal. You can concede a stroke anytime your opponent's ball is at rest, and you can remove it with a club, or your hand, or a plunger if you have one. You can concede a hole or the entire match at any time prior to the conclusion of the hole or match.

Since strokes are what make up your score, this is a good place to talk about the responsibilities you have regarding the reporting of your score. If you incur a penalty you're obliged to tell your opponent as soon as it happens, even if it means you have to walk over to him or wave him over to where you are. If you don't inform him immediately, then you are deemed under the Rules to have given him wrong information. Providing inaccurate information is in itself a penalty, so by not telling your opponent when you've incurred a penalty, you're actually incurring *two* penalties. There's no penalty if you correct your mistake before the guy's next shot. But if you finish the hole and then tell him you had penalty strokes, you automatically lose the hole, even if you had the lower score.

Actually, even when you haven't incurred a penalty, the guy you're playing always has a right to know, anytime during the hole, the number of strokes that you have played. Whenever he asks, you must correctly inform him how you stand at that moment. If he asks you and you tell him you lie three when you actually lie four (or vice versa) or you give any other incorrect information as to the number of strokes you've played, once he plays his next stroke you lose the hole. The moral of the story: If you make a mistake when telling your opponent your score, tell him as soon as you can. If there's ever a situation when you're not certain of the answer, replay the strokes (including penalty strokes) in your mind before answering.

The entire line of logic for this Rule continues after the hole is over. If you think you've erroneously reported your score for the completed hole, make sure you correct it before your opponent tees off on the next hole. If it's at the final hole of the match, make sure you tell him before you both leave the putting green. Here's an example of where this stuff gets tricky: You're playing a match and it goes into extra holes. On the first hole of the play-off you think you've holed out in six strokes and tell your opponent so. Your opponent has already played his sixth shot, so he concedes the match and the hole to you. On the way back to the clubhouse, you realize you incurred a penalty. What happens now? The match is over, right? Nope. Actually, whether you gave the wrong info knowingly or unwittingly, you lose the match.

Both you and your opponent are responsible for knowing the Rules. If your opponent asks you about a Rule and you tell him what you honestly believe and he proceeds under your interpretation of the Rule, he's making a big mistake. If you tell him the wrong thing, he assumes whatever penalties are handed out for proceeding in violation of the Rules. For example, if he says, "Can I take a drop here or do I get relief from this?" and you give him an honest but wrong answer and he wrongly proceeds, he gets whatever penalties result from his miscue.

Of course, as with every other situation in golf, you cannot knowingly lie about a situation in order to screw him up. If you do, you can lose the entire match, because the Rules Committee will disqualify you on the spot. In other words, you've got to be "correctly wrong." It's very important to pay attention to this in heated matches, because you never know when an opponent may level an accusation against you. Unless you're absolutely dead certain about a Rule when asked about it, your best bet is to say, "I don't know. Do what you think is right and we'll ask the Committee when we're finished."

Teeing ground: The starting place for the hole to be played. It is a rectangular area two club lengths in depth. The front and side of the rectangle are defined by the outside limits of two tee markers. A ball is outside the teeing ground when all of it lies outside the teeing ground.

If your opponent plays a tee shot from outside the teeing ground, you can make him play the shot over. There is no penalty, but you can rattle his cage by making him play over. You should watch for this—a lot of guys try to sneak ahead of the markers by a few inches.

Here's another thing that occurs on the teeing ground with great frequency. There you are on the tee, making one of your beautiful practice swings (for which you are so famous!), when you inadvertently nick the ball and send it sailing into the Sedona death cacti that border the tee. Your gleeful opponent insists you have to play the ball where it lies. Do you? No way. There's no penalty because you were not making what is considered a regulation stroke, which must be made with the clear intent to strike the ball. You're free to retee the ball and play away. So if this happens to you and your opponent asks, "Was that a practice swing?" simply assure him, very matter-of-factly, that it was. We don't recommend trying this after you've driven the ball 300 yards out of bounds. If you do this anywhere other than on the teeing ground, however, the stroke counts because the ball is in play.

Through the green: This is the entire area of the course with three exceptions: the teeing area, the putting green on the hole you're playing, and any hazards on the course.

Wrong ball: A wrong ball is any ball other than your ball in play or a provisional ball. There are other times when a ball is considered the wrong ball, but not in match play.

Here is a situation that happens a lot in match play: Both you and your opponent drive the ball a long way down the center of the fairway, and your ball comes to rest about five yards ahead of his but you don't know that. Without checking closely, you play his ball up onto the green and he steps up and plays your ball onto the green. When you get to the green, you both realize that you

WINNERS OF THE PGA CHAMPIONSHIP
AT MATCH PLAY

The PGA Championship is considered to be the weak sister of the four major championships, if for no other reason than it just seems to have a problem holding the interest of fans. It probably wouldn't if it were still conducted at match play, as it was from 1916 to 1957. This is especially true since the revival of the Ryder Cup has renewed interest in match play. Here's a look at the winners of the PGA Championship at match play. All finals were thirty-six holes.

1916: Jim Barnes, one-up over Jock Hutchison
1917–18: No matches, World War I
1919: Jim Barnes, 6 and 5 over Fred McLeod
1920: Jock Hutchison, one-up over J. Douglas Edgar
1921: Walter Hagen, 3 and 2 over Jim Barnes
1922: Gene Sarazen, 4 and 3 over Emmet French
1923: Gene Sarazen, 38 holes over Walter Hagen
1924: Walter Hagen, two-up over Jim Barnes
1925: Walter Hagen, 6 and 5 over William "Wild Bill" Mehlhorn
1926: Walter Hagen, 5 and 3 over Leo Diegel
1927: Walter Hagen, one-up over Joe Turnesa
1928: Leo Diegel, 6 and 5 over Al Espinosa
1929: Leo Diegel, 6 and 4 over Johnny Farrell
1930: Tommy Armour, one-up over Gene Sarazen
1931: Tom Creavy, 2 and 1 over Denny Shute

played the wrong ball. What happens? Whoever was the first to play the wrong ball loses the hole.

In stroke play you are always allowed to play a second ball if you're in doubt as to how to proceed during a Rules dispute or uncertainty. It's actually quite common in club-level events—you simply declare you're playing a second ball and play both balls until you hole them both out. You would keep both scores on your card until you consulted with the Rules Committee, which would

1932: Olin Dutra, 2 and 1 over Frank Walsh

1933: Gene Sarazen, 5 and 4 over Willie Goggin

1934: Paul Runyan, 38 holes over Craig Wood

1935: Johnny Revolta, 5 and 4 over Tommy Armour

1936: Denny Shute, 3 and 2 over Jimmy Thomson

1937: Denny Shute, 37 holes over Harold "Jug" McSpaden

1938: Paul Runyan, 8 and 7 over Sam Snead

1939: Henry Picard, 37 holes over Byron Nelson

1940: Byron Nelson, one-up over Sam Snead

1941: Vic Ghezzi, 38 holes over Byron Nelson

1942: Sam Snead, 2 and 1 over Jim Turnesa

1943: No matches, World War II

1944: Bob Hamilton, one-up over Byron Nelson

1945: Byron Nelson, 4 and 3 over Sam Byrd

1946: Ben Hogan, 6 and 4 over Ed "Porky" Oliver

1947: Jim Ferrier, 2 and 1 over Chick Harbert

1948: Ben Hogan, 7 and 6 over Mike Turnesa

1949: Sam Snead, 3 and 2 over Johnny Palmer

1950: Chandler Harper, 4 and 3 over Henry Williams, Jr.

1951: Sam Snead, 7 and 6 over Walter Burkemo

1952: Jim Turnesa, one-up over Chick Harbert

1953: Walter Burkemo, 2 and 1 over Felice Torza

1954: Chick Harbert, 4 and 3 over Walter Burkemo

1955: Doug Ford, 4 and 3 over Cary Middlecoff

1956: Jack Burke, Jr., 3 and 2 over Ted Kroll

1957: Lionel Hebert, 2 and 1 over Dow Finsterwald

determine which ball counts. In match play, you cannot play two balls; the dispute has to be settled on the spot. (This is not to be confused with a provisional ball, which is a ball you play when you're uncertain about the outcome of a particular shot.)

Another trick that an opponent may try sometime is claiming that since he didn't hit *your* ball, he didn't hit the *wrong* ball when he played some errant ball he found in the rough. He's wrong— any ball other than his is the wrong ball.

An important detail you should know about playing the wrong ball is that if you play the wrong ball from a hazard, there is *no penalty*. If it's your opponent's ball, he has to replace it. Either way, the time you took to play that shot does *not* count toward the five minutes you have to look for the ball.

In a four-ball match, if your partner plays the wrong ball, he is disqualified from that hole, but you can keep playing. If either of you plays the wrong ball in foursomes, you lose the hole.

MASTERS OF MATCH PLAY: SAM SNEAD

Who was the best match player ever? Lanny Wadkins? Ben Hogan? Old Tom Morris? There's no question those guys were good, but a solid case can be made that the best match player ever was Samuel Jackson Snead. If you're ever in a bar argument about the most talented player, put your money on Sam Snead. Today's young guns don't talk about Snead much, but he was a magnificent player. He was golf's version of Forrest Gump. Here's a glimpse at Snead's record as a player. He had eighty-one victories on the PGA Tour. That's the all-time record, and probably will never be touched. He had 135 worldwide victories. He won the Greater Greensboro Open *eight* times. He won two Masters, three PGA Championships, and one British Open. In the 1950 PGA Tour season, he won eleven tournaments. In 1979, at the Quad Cities Open, he became the youngest Tour player to shoot his age, when he shot sixty-seven in the third round. In the final round, he shot sixty-six. He played on seven Ryder Cup teams, and captained three. He played on four winning World Cup teams. He won his first professional Tour event in 1936 and his last in 1965. He won his last senior Tour event in 1982—forty-six years after his first Tour win.

And what about match play? Check out these records: Snead was 50–14 in PGA Championship play. That's a 78 percent winning percentage. He was 10-2-1 in Ryder Cup play. That's an 81 percent winning percentage.

Snead was by far the longest hitter of the ball in his day, and is perhaps the best natural athlete ever to play the game.

What you can learn from Sam Snead

Snead mastered the most difficult part of the golf swing, the transition from backswing to downswing.

The everyday golfer (that's you) struggles more with the transition phase of the swing than any other part. At this part of the swing the urge to kill the ball takes over, leading most people to grab on tighter with the hands and attempt to force a seemingly powerful arm swing.

Snead's swing was the opposite, and it demonstrated perfectly the notion of the body coiling for power and then slowly (in relative terms) unleashing it. What most everyday players don't realize about the golf swing is that the upper body doesn't do much in the way of initiating the action, particularly in the downswing.

At the start of his backswing, Snead took the club away at the same time that he started to turn his hips away from the target. Soon after, he let his lower body—his hips—take the lead and let his upper body go along for the ride. When he reached the top of his swing—when his hips could turn no more—he kept turning his shoulders, reaching and reaching until the club was well past parallel.

By the time Snead's club had completed its upward journey, his lower body had already begun to fire toward the target. There was a delay—a moment of suspended animation—when the club was neither moving back nor forward. But during that time, his hips were turning toward the target. This requires patience, and the knowledge that good things come to those who wait.

Once his upper body started to turn toward the ball, it picked up speed at a frightening pace. It didn't look fast because his tempo was so superb, but he had wound his body so tight that the far end of his human spring—the arms—started whipping toward the ball in an attempt to catch up to his lower body. The lower body was moving slower—as the center of a spring does—so it was possible for his arms to catch up. And his hands and arms and lower body did finally catch up at impact. The result was a powerful draw that sent the ball hurtling through the sky longer than any of his contemporaries.

7.

The Art of the
Gambling Match

Way back in 1912, the United States Golf Association (USGA) took its first stab at creating a system of handicapping so that players could compete against one another regardless of skill level. In other words, they made it a little easier for good players to make bad players feel like they had a chance in a bet. Which, of course, they don't—not usually, anyway. The fact is, the higher a player's handicap, the less likely he is to shoot a score reflective of it. Low handicappers usually shoot close to their handicap, while it's quite normal for high handicappers to shoot scores much higher than their handicaps.

The gambling match is the heart of golf. That may not sit too well with purists, but it's a fact. Most players don't care what they've *shot* as long as they win the money. Even the USGA acknowledges that playing for a few bucks is okay by them. It says so right in the Rules book: "The USGA does not object to participation in wagering among individual golfers or teams of golfers when participation in the wagering is limited to the players, the players may only wager on themselves or their teams, the sole source of all money won by players is advanced by the players, and the primary purpose is playing the game for enjoyment." We're not so sure where they got that last part, but they haven't played in our group recently. Anyway, at least you can rest easy now if you were wondering if your weekly Nassau might prevent you from playing on the next Walker Cup team.

There's an old bit about betting that goes something like this: Having a short putt to win the U.S. Open isn't pressure. Pressure is when you've made a ten-dollar bet and you only have one dollar in your pocket. Here are two rules to guide you through gambling games. First, always have enough money to cover any losses you might incur, unless you have a really, really fast car and you never plan on seeing the guy(s) again. (And you're pretty sure they won't come looking for you.) Second, make sure everyone, including you, understands the rules and procedures for the day. Every gambling game is different, and some of them can get confusing. So unless you've got deep pockets, make sure you know the nuances of the game *before you leave the first tee.*

Getting a Match Started

When you're betting, there is a negotiation process that takes place on the first tee, and it's all part of the fun and strategy of money matches. If you're not careful, you can lose the match right there on the first tee, and it happens more often than you think. The negotiating process is crucial to your chances out on the course—it's the only thing you can do to improve your odds of winning that has nothing to do with your talent as a player.

There are two types of first-tee negotiations, the kind with people you know and the kind with people you don't know. If you're negotiating with people you know, it's easier to make the process work in your favor. If you're negotiating with people you don't know, our advice is simple: Keep the bet small. If someone starts egging you toward a bigger bet than you're comfortable making, bow out gracefully or brace yourself for an ugly match. Guys who like to play for significant stakes with strangers are usually pretty sure they're going to win, even if they have to cheat.

It probably goes without saying, but your opponent's handicap is like underwear—sometimes it's clean and sometimes it stinks. If you're the low handicapper in a group, there is one cardinal rule to negotiating: You should do all the talking and ask all the questions, because the lowest handicapper in a group is at the biggest disadvantage since he has to give shots to the other players.

Since we're assuming you have some knowledge of your opponent in a betting game, here are a few tips on getting an edge on the first tee:

- Be the first one to bring up the idea of a bet and suggest amounts in your comfort range. Most guys are too proud to say a wager is too high, so set it as high as *you* want it to be.
- Ask a lot of questions about how your opponents have been playing lately. A lousy money player won't be able to resist telling you if he's playing well.
- If you get asked how you're playing, be evasive or lie. We don't want to cause a disruption in your moral standards, but hey, you're gambling here, pal. Everyone lies when it comes to gambling. If you're not comfortable lying, just shrug your shoulders a lot.
- The object of the negotiation is to get the other guys to play with less strokes than their handicap entitles them to, and maybe to squeak out one or two extra for yourself. If your opponents tell you they've been playing well, that opens the door for you to work them down a stroke or two. As for you, your standard answer to questions about how you've been playing is, "I can't even keep the damned ball on the course," even if you shot 72 the day before.
- Whenever you're the low handicapper, negotiate an "adjustment" at the turn. This means that after nine holes, the two

of you will agree to adjust the high handicapper's strokes for the back nine to roughly match what he shot on the front nine. This will keep you from getting sandbagged.

- If you're the low handicapper, try to get the guy who gets the most strokes as your partner. It'll eat at the two guys in the middle that they have to give up a few strokes, too.
- Make sure you know where the strokes fall in the match, and don't forget. Mark the scorecard and look at it before every hole. This is another reason why you want the high handicapper—he'll probably get more strokes over the closing holes.
- Of course, people are great at making up excuses as to why you should give them more shots. Here are a few we've heard over the years:

> "I haven't played in a long time."
> "I put my daughter's contact lenses in by mistake."
> "I'm not feeling well."
> "I was up all night."
> "I've got a wooden leg."

Okay, we made that last one up. The point is, you shouldn't believe any excuses when it comes to betting on golf—they're probably lying and if they're not, it isn't your problem. It's been written that the night before a big match, Walter Hagen's valet and caddie used to take his tuxedo, roll it up into a ball, jump up and down on it, and throw it against the wall so it would get wrinkled. Meanwhile, Sir Walter got a good night's sleep. The next day, Hagen would show up late for his match wearing the wrinkled tux, making it seem as if he'd been out all night partying. While he pardoned himself to change into "fresh" clothes, his opponents started to think about how easy it would be to beat the hungover Hagen. All this by way of saying you have to be prepared for anything on the first tee.

Another thing you have to get straight before you start the match is how you're going to "play" the ball. Are you going to play it "down," which means you play it as it lies at every point during the match? Are you going to play "winter rules," which means you can adjust your lie in the fairway? Or are you going to play "roll 'em everywhere," which means you can improve your lie everywhere but in a hazard? Basically, the better player you are the more you should insist on playing the ball down. Most high handicappers don't like to play the ball down and almost routinely improve their lie. The effect of playing the ball down can really be seen in the short game, where high handicappers are accustomed to moving the ball all over the place so they have a nice, cushy lie from which to chip or pitch. If you make a high handicapper play the ball down, he'll have a hard time playing to his handicap. On the other hand, if *you* are the high handicapper, you may want to bargain to "roll 'em everywhere."

The conditions of play on the day of a match are of major importance. If it's wet and soggy, short hitters are going to have a tough go of it. Because everyone's ball is going to plug into the soggy ground, the short hitter is going to lose about 30 percent of the distance on his tee shots due to the lack of roll. (Thirty percent is our estimate based on what we see at our golf schools.) This means he's going to be hitting a lot of long shots into the greens— shots he's not capable of playing. So if you're playing a short hitter on a soggy day, up the bet, partner!

Wind is the other big factor that affects a player's game. Wind exacerbates any spin on the ball, and most high handicappers slice the ball, which means they're going to have a long day. Same goes for the Bomber, who hits it all over the lot—his bad shots are going to be even more off-target than usual. Also, a player who normally hits the ball low or *can* hit the ball low is better off than the player who hits the ball real high. Taking any of these things into consideration on the first tee may allow you to be more aggressive with your betting.

High-handicap players are usually not very good putters, which means on fast greens they're going to struggle. You should ask your opponent what type of greens he normally plays on. If he says they're average speed or slow, and you know the ones you're about to play are fast, ask him if he brought his ATM card with him.

Of all the mistakes it's possible to make when betting, one of the most foolish is to have a side match against your partner. You've got to decide if you're going to play against your opponents or each other. If you want an individual match, have it against one of your opponents. If you have an individual match with your partner, it changes strategies, i.e., one of you might try a risky shot (and fail) because you want to win your side match. If you're playing with a partner, you should be pulling for each other, not against each other.

Finally, don't be afraid to be creative with your bets. There is an old story about a big money match at Royal Liverpool in England. The match was between a scratch player and a six handicapper. Rather than taking his handicap strokes, the six handicapper negotiated the right to holler "Boo!" three times during the match. Well, he played it smart and saved them until, at the thirteenth hole, with the match all square, he yelled "Boo!" at the top of his opponent's backswing. He scared the bejesus out of the opponent, who fired a wild drive into trouble. He lost the hole and the match. The six handicapper never had to use the rest of his "Boo's" because the fear that he might was more powerful than actually using them.

The Games

Nassau: The most basic bet in golf is called a Nassau, which is so named for the club in New York that is believed to be the place where the bet originated.

The Nassau divides an eighteen-hole match into three separate bets of equal value, one for the front nine, one for the back nine,

PICKING A VENUE THAT GIVES YOU
THE ADVANTAGE

Let's say you play with the same guys all the time, and one day after a round you're sitting in the grillroom and someone says, "We've been playing the same five-dollar Nassau for ten years. Why don't we try something different for a change?" This is your cue. What you want to do is suggest a match for a higher wage at a course different than the one you normally play. You suggest the venue. If you're a Machine, pick a long, tight course. If you're a Bomber or a Magician, pick a long, wide-open course. If you're a short guy, pick a course that is known for being windy—your ball will be affected the same as everyone else's, but *you* won't get blown around as much, and you'll be more comfortable over your shots, especially putts.

If one of the guys you're playing against is really tall, pick a course that is very hilly. Tall guys have a tough time with their leg action and footwork when playing from uneven lies. If you're the best putter in the group, pick a course with fast greens or get on a course near water or mountains, where the general terrain affects putts in a way the bad putters won't understand. If you're a lousy putter, suggest a course that has slow, flat greens. This will kill the good putters, who will have trouble hitting the ball hard enough and might tend to overread the greens, playing for subtle breaks that aren't there.

Maybe you're a good sand player. If you are, pick a course with lots of bunkers. If you're a short hitter, pick a short course that doesn't have a lot of forced carries. You get the idea.

and one for the entire eighteen holes. Once the front nine is complete, the outcome of the front-nine portion of the bet cannot be altered. So, if you win the front nine two up, you've won that part of the bet no matter what happens on the back nine. If you go on to win the back nine, you sweep all three bets. If you lose the back nine, the outcome of the bet for the overall match depends on the margin by which you lose. If you lose the back nine two down, the overall match is halved and no money changes hands. If you lose the back nine one down, you still win the overall match one up, so you win a total of one point.

There are two fairly common twists to the Nassau match. The first is called a "carryover," which means that the value of holes halved is carried along until someone wins a hole. So, for example, if the first two holes are halved and you win the third hole, you're three up rather than one up. The second twist is called a "press," which is the establishment of minimatches within the larger matches. Typically, a press is asked for when either side falls two down. If the press is accepted, a new match begins from that point on through the remainder of the specified match. Here's an example: You and your partner are two down after four holes and you'd like to try to make up for that. You decide to press, so you say to your opponents, "We'll press you on the front nine." That means from the fourth hole to the ninth hole, a new match is in effect. The original match is still going on, however—the press doesn't wipe that out. Still, if you lose the front nine one down, but win your press bet (holes four through nine) one up, you've canceled out any gains made by your opponents. When asking for a press, you have to be specific; you can press for the front nine, the back nine, or the entire match.

If you don't know what you're doing, presses can get messy and you can lose more money than you bargained for. It's always a good idea to get the details of pressing worked out on the first tee. Sometimes, players agree upon "automatic" presses, which typically go into effect any time a side falls two behind in any element of the match. On a bad day, that can turn into a lot of dough. You also need to be clear about whether or not the presses have to be accepted (in nonautomatic matches). In other words, if you and your partner press, does the other team have to allow you, or can it refuse? You can do it either way, but you have to decide before you start playing. If you don't like the idea of possibly winning the first seventeen holes and having it all wiped out by a press to "get even" on the last hole, our advice is to leave the option of refusal open. Unless you're extremely familiar with your opponent, you should avoid automatic presses. If you think the conditions favor you, and you know the opponent like an old dog, then go ahead and ask for automatic presses. Just think twice before doing this when you're playing someone on their own course under perfect conditions, where they know every blade of grass. You can get buried in a hurry under those circumstances.

Skins: One of the most popular bets for group match play is a game called "skins." A lot of golfers are familiar with this one because of the annually televised Skins Game, which pits four PGA Tour players against each other. This made-for-television event differs from the millions of skins games played by everyday golfers in one very noteworthy way: The guys on TV aren't playing for their own money. Here's how it works. The low ball on the hole wins. If there is a tie for low ball, everyone ties, and the point is carried forward to the next hole. So if the first four holes are halved and then one guy wins the fifth hole outright, he picks up five skins from each of the other three players. In a typical skins game, the value of each skin increases as the match wears on—the first six holes are the least valuable skins, holes seven through twelve are usually worth twice what the first six holes are, and holes thirteen through eighteen are worth twice what the preceding six holes are worth. At the end, each player totals up his money earned, making sure to use the right amounts on various holes. For example, if you play a skins game where the first six holes are worth one dollar, the second six two dollars, and the third six four dollars, you have to do the proper math. So, if you won the third, fourth, seventh, tenth, and seventeenth holes (with no carryovers), your earnings are ten dollars. You owe anyone who has more than you the difference between his total and yours, and anyone who has less than you owes you the difference between your total and theirs. This game is so much fun because it's match play against three other people at the same time and because if you tank on any given hole, there are two other guys who can save your butt. Skins also rewards the player who plays best down the home stretch since there tends to be a lot of carryovers and the last six holes are worth the most money.

Wolf (also known as Hawk): This is a great game to set up if you have to give away so many shots you don't want to play a team game. To explain it, we'll assume there are four players, A, B, C, and D. Everyone plays to his full handicap. Before the game starts, you have to set an order of play from the tees. For the sake of this example, we'll assume A, B, C, and D have decided to play in that order.

On the first tee, A hits first. After he hits, he prepares to select a partner for the hole. If B hits a good drive and A likes his prospects, he must select B as his partner on the spot—before C hits his drive. If A picks B, they are partners for that hole only versus C and D.

Perhaps A isn't overly fond of B's drive and wants to wait to see if he can get a better partner on the hole. Then C hits his drive. If A likes the look of C's drive, he must select him as his partner before D plays from the tee. If A does not select B or C, he is automatically left with D as a partner. The partnerships last only for one hole, and the points won are all individual points.

Now here's the fun part. Anytime a player is first on the tee, he may elect to declare himself the wolf. When a player does so, it means he is going to take on all three players by himself. When a player declares himself the wolf, all points available on the hole are doubled. This can be a real hoot when there is a bunch of carryovers on the line. There is one catch to being the wolf: You must declare it immediately after you play your drive, before the next player hits. Once the next guy hits, you can no longer declare yourself the wolf, and must pick a partner. When playing this game, remember not to go daydreaming on your tee. You may miss some good drives and possible partners and get stuck with the last guy . . . who will probably hit into a cluster of rare Caribbean stinging paralyzer plants.

Here's the order of play from the tees: first hole—A, B, C, D; second hole—B, C, D, A; third hole—C, D, A, B; fourth hole—D, A, B, C; fifth hole—A, B, C, D. And so forth. When you get to the ninth hole, the player with the fewest number of points gets the tee. At the tenth, you return to the same order that you started the front nine, regardless of who had the tee at the ninth. On the eighteenth hole, the tee once again belongs to the guy with the fewest points.

All the points in wolf are worth the same amount, so to figure out the payoff everyone just adds up his points won and pays out the difference to each player. Don't forget to figure in those carryovers and doubled points from holes when a player declares himself the wolf.

Junk: Junk are individual side bets you can throw into the mix to keep things lively. All junk doesn't have to have the same value, but it helps to keep things straight if all junk points are worth the same amount. Junk can add up to some serious cash if you carry them over.

Some junk you can play:

- Natural birdies.
- Natural eagles. (If you play these, you should probably be on the PGA Tour.)
- Greenies. A greenie is the closest ball on the green on any par three. To win the bet, you have to make par or better. Balls on the fringe don't count.
- Sandies. If you get up and down from a bunker to save par or better, that's a sandy. If you go from a fairway bunker to a greenside bunker and then get up and down for a par, that's a double sandy, and worth twice the points.
- Poleys. Any putt longer than the flagpole that is holed gets a point.

- Barkys. Any player who hits a tree and still makes par wins a point.
- Bingle Bangle Bongle. Points are awarded to the player on the green in the fewest strokes, the closest to the hole once all balls are on the green, and the first to hole out.

Vegas: This is the king of crazy games. Bring an armored car to escort you home, and be careful about the value you assign the points. When playing Vegas, you have a partner. The player with the lowest score wins the hole for his team. Let's use our friends A, B, C, and D to demonstrate how it works. A and B are partners, and C and D are partners. On the first hole, A makes a three and B makes a five. On the same hole, C makes a four and D makes an eight. The team score for the hole is determined by making a two-digit number out of the team's individual scores, placing the low ball first. In this example, A and B's team score would be 35 and C and D's team score would be 48. You keep score like that all day, and at the end of the round, the team with the highest number owes the team with the lower number the difference between the two numbers.

This game does have a twist. (Don't they all.) If you and your partner both make birdie on the same hole, your opponents have to transpose the order of their numbers, placing the higher one first. If you and your partner both make birdie, you can only hope that one of your opponents makes a big number. If he makes a ten, you're talking a triple-digit point win on a single hole.

Playing a Feathered Shot

Every good gambling golfer knows how to play a "feather" shot, and you should, too. It's golf's version of *The Sting*. A feather shot is played with much more club than is called for by the distance— *if* the club were hit at its full value. But it's not, which is how you sucker your opponent.

MASTERS OF MATCH PLAY:
LEE TREVINO

Legend has it that, as a young man in Texas, Lee Trevino played money matches using a Dr. Pepper bottle as his club. (He wasn't too crazy. He covered it in tape.) Since no one could believe he would beat them with a soda bottle, Trevino used to win a lot of cash.

When he hit the pro Tour, no one really knew who he was. He didn't have a fabulous amateur career like Arnold Palmer and Jack Nicklaus, and he wasn't a college star like Tiger Woods and Phil Mickelson were before they hit the big time. Trevino was just a self-taught scrapper with a lot of guts and even more nerve.

Trevino qualified for the U.S. Open in 1967 at Baltusrol, and quietly finished fifth while no one was looking. He won $6,000, which was enough to bankroll him on the PGA Tour in 1968. He made it back to the Open that year and won it at Oak Hill. People got a kick out of Trevino—he walked fast and talked fast and often. He had a nice self-deprecating way about him. And he had a game, working the ball in a manner other players only could in their dreams—left to right mostly, but he could move it any way he chose.

In 1971, Trevino won the Open again, this time at Merion, and he did it by beating Jack Nicklaus in an eighteen-hole play-off. A month later he won the British Open, becoming one of only five men to win both Opens in the same year. (Bobby Jones, Gene Sarazen, Ben Hogan, and Tom Watson are the others.) The next year, 1972, he won the British Open again. Along the way, he tossed in a couple of PGA Championships (1974 and 1984) to round things out.

Trevino loved a game. In the 1987 Skins Game, Trevino aced the seventeenth hole at PGA West, a hole known as Alcatraz because it is surrounded by water. That shot helped him cart home $310,000. He was just as tough in the Ryder Cup, compiling a 17-7-6 record. In fact, Trevino made the team the first year he was eligible for it. Nicklaus made the team the same year for the first time (1969), but by that time he'd been on Tour for seven years and won five major championships! Captain Sam

Snead liked Trevino's game so much he sent him out in all six matches. (Another Ryder Cup rookie that year is well-known gamer Raymond Floyd. He actually has a losing Ryder Cup record, however, at 12-16-3.) If the PGA Championship had been played at match play during Trevino's prime, he might have won every year.

What you can learn from Lee Trevino

No one knows when golfers first started to talk about "working the ball," but Lee Trevino didn't just work a ball—he gave it a career. If you're not familiar with the phrase, "working the ball" means to make it take any flight other than straight or with an ordinary trajectory. Being able to work the ball is vital to truly being a player who is never out of the hole. Playing a superb recovery shot when your opponent thinks you're in trouble is the quickest way to plunge a knife into his momentum.

Here are the basic rules for working the ball:

- It's easier to curve the ball from left to right with less lofted clubs. So if you want to fade the ball, take less club and choke down about a half inch.
- It's easier to curve the ball from right to left with more lofted clubs. Remember that if you're trying to hook a ball around a tree and back into play.
- It's difficult to play any sort of controlled curve from a heavy lie in the rough, so you're better off not trying it if you're in the spinach.
- A faded ball will run less when it hits the ground, so allow for it. A drawn ball will run more than a fade.
- Any controlled curved shot is made easier with a shorter swing, so it's not a bad idea to always take extra club and choke down.
- The basics for playing a fade or controlled slice:
  —Aim the lead edge of the clubface at the point you want the ball to finish up.
  —Align your body left of that point—your shoulders, hips, and feet. How much left? Aim them at the highest point on your

desired curve—the spot at which you want the ball to stop going left and start going right.

—Play the ball slightly right of the center of your body.

—Through impact, hang on a little tighter with your left hand.

- The basics for playing a draw or controlled hook:

—Aim the lead edge of the clubface at your target.

—Aim your body points right of your target using the same rules
as for the fade. Aim your body at the point where you want the
ball to stop moving right and start moving left.

—Play the ball slightly left of the center of your body.

- If you want to play a low punch shot from the trees, play the ball
back in your stance and tighten your grip with your left hand. Keep
your left wrist firm through impact. Note: If your ball is in the trees
and resting on leaves or pine needles, don't ground your club. The
ball might move.

- If the ball is sitting on a hill and it's higher than your feet, it is going
to curve from right to left when you hit it. You can aim right, but
don't aim where a straight shot will put you in trouble. When
addressing the ball, choke up on the club and stand up a little
straighter in the knees. How much you adjust depends on the
severity of the hill.

- If the ball is sitting on a hill and it's lower than your feet, it is going
to curve from left to right when you strike it. If you aim left to allow
for it, don't aim where a straight ball will get you in trouble. Lower
yourself to the ball by a combination of extra knee flex and extra
tilt from the hips.

- If the ball is sitting on an uphill lie, i.e., your body is angled away from
the target, it is going to fly left and higher than normal, so take more
club. It's not going to curve, it's going to be a straight pull. At
address, lean with the hill, not against it.

- If the ball is sitting on a downhill lie, i.e., your body is leaning toward
the target, the ball is going to be pushed to the left, fly lower, and
run longer, so allow for it. At address, lean with the hill.

- If you need to hit a super-severe hook or slice around a tree, you may want to adjust your grip. If you turn your left hand to the right on the club so that your left thumb is well right of the center of the grip, it will help create a severe hook. The ball won't get very high, so we recommend this only as a trouble shot. If you turn your left thumb to the left of center, it will create a severe slice. This will be a weak shot, but if you need to hit a short banana ball, it might help.

For the feather shot to work, you have to make certain your opponent knows what club you're hitting. About the only way you can ensure this is to play the shot on a par three, when he's standing right next to you. (There's no point in playing a feathered shot on a driving hole.) It's easy to make sure he knows what club you're using. First, you can tell him. But unless he's a complete idiot, he'll probably know something is up if you do that. (Obviously, we're not talking about a match in competition, because telling him what you hit would be against the Rules.) Your best bet is to make a big production out of choosing a club. Take a club out of your bag and walk over to the ball. Then walk back and take another club. This should get him looking. If not, do it again. Eventually, he'll be looking in your bag to see what club you have in your hand.

Once he's hooked, you have to execute the shot. But this is no problem for you because you've practiced it, and you know you can throttle back enough on this club to make it go the right distance. And you practiced it for a specific hole on the course, based on its distance. So, let's say that hole is 160 yards and you usually hit your five-wood about 190 yards. Your opponent may not know how far you can hit a five-wood, but he does know that almost anyone can hit it farther than 160 yards.

So, after much ado, you select your five-wood and your opponent sees you. You step up to the ball and he's watching intently. You swing and the ball takes off looking like any other shot, and it lands on the green. Your opponent gets up with his five-wood or equivalent club and sends his ball flying over the green into the forest of Death. How did you do it? Simple. You played the ball in your normal ball position, made a smooth, slow swing, and you made two adjustments. First, you swung the club using mostly your arms. Second, you limited your body turn, only turning about three-quarters as much as you usually do.

You can also accomplish the same thing by teeing the ball up slightly higher than normal, so that you hit it high on the clubface. The ball will fly about one club shorter.

Seem a little complicated? In that case, just switch your head-covers around, so that the numbers on the covers and the clubs don't match. Then, when you select a club to play, toss the cover on the ground near your opponent's feet. This will divert his attention away from your club, and he'll see the number on the cover. After you hit your shot, keep your hand over the bottom of your club as you walk back to your bag. Wait until he's setting up to the ball to put back your cover. Then laugh all the way to the bank.

8.

Talking the Talk:
The Lingo of Match Play

The language of match play and the language of betting are intermingled to the point where it is impossible to make a distinction between the two. It's easy to understand the reason why; almost every match has a bet riding on it and almost every golf bet is settled at match play. There is also a simple reason why you should understand the language of match play and betting: If you don't, you'll end up getting taken to the cleaners more frequently than Wayne Newton's tuxedo. Now pay attention.

action: Collectively, all the bets made in any match. So if you want to start some trouble on a slow day, just ask if anyone "feels like a little action." For reasons that are incomprehensible, the word *action* is always preceded by the word *little*. Little or not, when you get yourself some "action," you've got yourself a game.

air press: An air press is a single-hole press (see *press*) that cannot be refused. It can be made by any player against his opponent while the opponent's ball is in the air. It doesn't matter how long the ball is in the air—if it hits a pebble on the green and bounces into the air, that's long enough to air press. There's only one rule when you're playing air presses—they have to be called before the ball hits the ground. There's no limit to the number that you can call on a hole. The idea behind the bet is to call a press when your opponent's ball is heading for trouble.

all square: When a match is tied at any point, it is "all square."

alternate shot: A more everyday term for "foursomes." In alternate shot, you and your partner alternate hitting a single ball until it is holed. One player tees off on the odd-numbered holes, and the other tees off on the even-numbered holes.

automatics *or* automatic presses: A press is a bet that begins a new match within a match. Automatic presses are agreed to prior to the round, and it means that any team or player that falls two down must press the original bet. This type of press is sometimes referred to as "two-down automatics" or simply "automatics."

away: A reference to the ball and the player farthest from the hole at any given moment. This is an important word in match play, because the player who is away is, under the Rules, entitled to play first. So, if you're on the back of a green and you're fifty feet from the hole, and your opponent is on the fringe about twenty feet from the hole, it is your turn to play. If he gives you the old, "I'm going to come up," or "I'm just going to play up," meaning he's about to play out of turn, you should say, "No, I'm away. I'll play." Simply put, away means just what it says—*away.* There are no distinctions made regarding *where* the ball lies around the greens, so a ball in a bunker could very well be closer to the hole than a ball on the fringe or the green, especially if it's a large green.

back *or* **back nine:** In an eighteen-hole match, the second nine holes. In a Nassau match, one element of the bet is for the back nine only.

best ball *or* **better ball:** A two-man team match that features the two low balls of each team against each other in a match-play format. For example, you make a four on a hole and your partner makes a five. Your opponents make a five and a six. Your team wins the hole based on your ball (a four) versus the opposition's low ball (a five). The two higher scores are irrelevant to the score of the match. For betting purposes, this format is sometimes altered to the best score of three balls versus the single ball of an outstanding player. In its standard form (two against two) this type of match is sometimes referred to as a four-ball.

bisque: This is a floating handicap stroke that you are allowed to use at any point in the match. It's something you might want to try to negotiate if you think you're overmatched. The bisque is in addition to your normal handicap strokes. The only catch is, you have to declare your intention to use it before play begins on the hole.

blood *or* **no blood:** When a hole is tied in match play, the competitors often refer to the halve as "no blood," as in "we fought but no blood was drawn." Since games sometimes get confusing and players occasionally lose track of the proceedings, it's not uncommon to inquire, "Was there any blood there?" at the completion of a hole, or to simply offer up, "No blood?"

bogey competition: This is a fun style of pseudo–match play for a large group of players. There was a time in golf when the word *bogey* meant a good score, not a bad one. (Bogey was the standard of good play for an average golfer. The concept of par was introduced later on as the standard of *expert* play.) As such, bogey competitions were held on a regular basis. The format works like this: You play your own ball in a match versus Colonel Bogey, who is a very consistent player—he scores one more than par on every hole. The winner of the competition is whoever beats the good colonel by the greatest margin. It's a good way to play on a day when you have a dozen or so players and everyone kicks a few bucks into a pot for the winner.

breakfast ball: Another way of saying "mulligan." Serious betters don't deal with this sort of stuff, which is really just an excuse for not being ready to play.

bye: If you're playing in a club tournament, the low qualifiers from medal play will sometimes be awarded a bye in the early rounds of match play. This means you automatically advance to a later round without having to play a match.

bye holes: When a match is decided before the eighteenth hole, those holes remaining unplayed are referred to as the bye holes. In competitive golf, once the possibility of an overall halve has been eliminated, the players stop playing and walk into the clubhouse.

carryover: In betting games, the value of a hole(s) tied is added to the value of the subsequent hole or holes until someone wins outright. If you're playing in a match with carryovers, they are important, because no hole is truly halved—the value is just tacked on to the next hole.

Chapman scoring: This match-play format isn't used all that frequently, but it's a fun one to try if you're bored with the same old same old. Here's how it works: You and your partner both hit drives. For the second shot, you switch; you hit his ball and he hits your ball. After the second shot, you select a single ball (the one in the best position), and play alternate shot from that point until you hole out.

concede: Only in match play can a shot or hole be conceded. You can concede a hole or a shot to your opponent at any time. Typically, you should wait until he's within a few inches of the hole. To sound like a real player, you don't want to say, "I'll concede that putt to you." Instead, you can say, "Pick it up," or "That's good," or "Take it away." All three are acceptable ways of conceding the next shot. Another way is just to knock it back to your man after he's putted. (In the 1993 Ryder Cup at The Belfry, Jose Maria Olazabal conceded the last hole and the match to Raymond Floyd by simply jerking his thumb toward the sky as if to say, "Pick it up.") A few things to remember about conceding *anything* in match play: Once you do it, you can't take it back. And if it's offered to you, you cannot refuse it. But why would you?

desert rules: This is one of those things you have to agree upon before starting a match. In the Southwest, where many courses wind through desert, a hole usually consists of a tee box, fairway, and green. If you miss that fairway, there are a whole bunch of reasons why you don't want to be tramping around looking for your ball, such as cacti, rattlesnakes, and tarantulas to name a few. Accordingly, some players declare desert rules on the first tee. This means rather than playing your ball as a lost ball and returning to the original spot to play another ball, you simply play the desert as if it is a lateral hazard, i.e., you take a penalty stroke and drop the ball where it crossed into the desert. It helps speed up play and prevent trips to the hospital.

dormie: A match is dormie when one player is ahead by the same number of holes remaining in the match. In other words, the player who is ahead will win if any of the remaining holes are halved. The player leading the match is said to be "dormie," combined with the number of holes he is ahead. For example, if Bob is three up with three holes to play, he is said to be "dormie three."

double dip: In some matches, a natural birdie on a hole is rewarded with a predetermined amount of money. If you and your partner both make birdie on the same hole, that's referred to as a double dip—your opponents have to dip into their wallets twice.

down: This has two applications in match play. If you're losing a match, you're "down" by the number of holes by which you trail. So if you're losing by two holes, you're "two down." You can also use it to describe your preference for playing the ball as it lies for the entire round, i.e., "Let's play 'em down today, boys."

down and dirty: This means the same thing as playing the ball "down."

even: A match that is tied is sometimes referred to as "even."

feathered shot: A feathered shot occurs when a player hits the ball with the intention of producing a shot that will travel a great deal less distance than that normally produced by a full-blooded swing with the same club. This type of shot is hit for the sole purpose of fooling your opponent in match play. It works because it is legal for your opponent to look in your bag to see what club you've hit. A feathered shot creates a false impression of the distance to the hole and, when the tactic works, causes your opponent to hit his ball over the green. For the technique involved in hitting a feather shot, see the chapter on gambling.

first on wins: Some players feel that they'll win almost any hole when they are the first ones on the green, and as such usually play for the center of the green on approach shots. For certain types of players, mostly Machines, it is a fairly sound notion. But for

Bombers and Magicians, it might not be, since it goes against their natural style.

four-ball match: You'll rarely hear this used in the United States with the exception of Ryder Cup play. A four-ball is a better-ball contest between two two-man teams, the low ball on each team being matched to determine the outcome of a hole. The way to keep from confusing this with "foursomes" (alternate shot) is to remember that in a four-ball match, there are four balls in play.

foursomes: This occurs when two-man teams play a single ball, alternating shots. Tee shots are played by an individual on alternate holes.

front: Short for "front nine," it's the first of the three-part Nassau bet.

game: When someone asks if you want to play a game, they're asking if you want to make a bet.

get-evens: A sucker bet that allows the losing side a chance at double or nothing on the eighteenth hole. It's probably a dumber bet to make than it is to accept. If you make it, you've been losing all day and there's no point in adding fuel to the fire.

get one: This can mean two things. If someone tells you that you "get one here," it means you get a handicap stroke on that hole. If you tell your partner you need to "get this one" or "we need to get this one here," that means it's an important hole in the match, and you really, really want to win it.

gimme: Slang for a short putt that is conceded, or at least a putt of the length where a player expects it should be conceded.

give shots: This means your opponent is getting handicap strokes and you're not. In other words, you're "giving" him an advantage on certain holes.

golf lawyer: Basically, this guy is a cheater. He tries to use his supposed knowledge of the Rules to swindle unsuspecting opponents. If you're in a match, remember that just because someone *sounds* like he knows what he's talking about, doesn't mean it's true. Also, keep in mind that often the guys like Ted Knight's character in *Caddyshack* are the ones who cheat this way, hiding behind the guise of propriety.

good *or* that's good: When you say these words, you're conceding a putt. So don't say them unless you mean them.

good good: This is what happens when you get two lousy putters who both face short putts to halve a hole. A "good good" exchange means that both players simultaneously concede before either one plays the putt. It's a good way to make sure you don't lose any ground, and also a good way not to gain any. Might be smart on a hole very early in a match.

go to school: If your partner has a putt along a similar line to yours, you should encourage him to watch your putt so he can learn about the speed and the break on the putt, i.e., so he can go to school on your putt. Another time you should think about this in team play is when you're out of contention on a hole and one of your opponents has a putt along the same line as you. In this case, you should just pick up your ball and move on to the next tee. This will deny your opponent the chance to go to school on your putt.

greenies: A side bet within a match, contested only on par threes. The point is awarded to the player whose ball is on the green and closest to the hole. The fringe doesn't count. And you have to make at least a par. Three putt and you don't get the greenie. If no one hits the green, the point carries over to the next par three.

grocery: The money up for grabs in a betting match is sometimes referred to as the "grocery." The implied thought is that some golfers are stupid enough to gamble away their grocery money.

gross: Your score on a hole before handicap strokes are deducted.

halve: When a hole or match is tied, it is halved. In team match play like the Ryder Cup, a halved match is worth one-half point.

ham and egg: A quality of a partnership that means one guy plays well while the other one is playing poorly. Ham-and-egg partners are tough to beat from a psychological standpoint because at least one of them comes through in the clutch.

handicap strokes: Strokes that are deducted from the gross score to determine the net score on a hole. In any given match, the player with the lowest handicap doesn't get any handicap strokes, and the other three players "play off of his ball." This means they get the difference between his handicap and their own. So, when a seven handicap is in a match with a nine handicap, an eleven handicap, and a fifteen handicap, he gives them two shots, four shots, and eight shots respectively.

high-low: A Nassau match where the high and low balls of a partnership are matched against the high and low balls of their opponents, and two points are available on each hole. An example: You make a four on a hole and your partner makes a five. Your opponents make a five and a six. You win two points because your high ball was better than their high ball (five versus six) and your low ball was lower than their low ball (four versus five). A good format to choose if the players in a group have widely varied handicaps.

honor: The order of play from the tee is known as the "honor." On the first hole, a coin is usually flipped to determine who will play first. On the subsequent tees, the team or player who won the previous hole has the right to play first.

I got high, you take low: This is a joke made in a high-low match by one partner to another. If you're really screwing up, you say, "I got high, you take low," and that means that he's pretty much on his own for that hole.

individuals: Most betting matches are team matches, which often is not enough to satisfy the devoted gambler who wants all the action he can lay his hands on. Under such circumstances, he may play separate matches versus the individuals in the group. Some players even play individuals against their own partners, which we think is a dumb idea because it can divide the team emotionally and cause strategy changes that are bad for the team.

in my pocket *or* in the linen: This is how you tell your partner and opponent that you're picking up on a hole, meaning you won't finish the hole and therefore remove yourself from contention. Once you do it, you can't change your mind.

inside the leather: Some players use the grip on the putter as a reference point to determine whether a putt should be conceded or not. Under this notion, any putt inside the bottom end of the grip of the putter is deemed good. It's a rather fainthearted way of playing if you ask us.

junk: A series of small bets, such as greenies and poleys, within a larger match are collectively referred to as "junk." (A poley is any putt holed that is longer than the flagstick [the pole].)

kicks and throws: A betting game that allows each player to kick the ball twice and throw the ball twice during the course of a match. This is done without penalty.

leaf rule: This falls into the same category as desert rules. In the fall, when leaves are all over the ground, any ball that is deemed lost due to the leaves can be replaced by dropping a ball near the spot where the players think it was. This is not an actual Rule, and if you decide to use it, it has to be used when there is no other possible explanation for the whereabouts of the ball. In other words, if your ball is headed toward a hazard, it's unlikely you're going to get away with invoking the leaf rule.

level: Just another way of saying a match is tied.

lift, clean, and place: An important condition of play to be aware of if you're in a big match. If the ground is very muddy, the club may decide that lift, clean, and place rules are in effect. That means before any shot you can lift the ball, clean it, and then place it on the ground rather than dropping it.

local rules: Local rules are not part of the Rules of golf, but they are allowed for in the Rules. Local rules are established by the club to deal with situations that are unique to that course. For example, a course may declare wetlands as out of play. It's a smart move to familiarize yourself with any local rules before you begin a match. It's easy to do—just ask the pro or the starter.

lockjaw: What a player has when he won't concede even the shortest of putts.

low gross: A stroke-play bet within a match-play match. It's a single wager awarded to the player who shoots the lowest gross score.

match cards: The match-play style means of determining a winner in a stroke-play event. The winner is determined by comparing the scorecards, match-play style. The first person or team to win a hole outright wins the event. Sometimes cards are matched starting with the first hole, and sometimes they are matched beginning with the eighteenth hole and working backward.

mulligan: No doubt named for a golfer with a hangover, this is a freebie second tee shot at the first hole. If everyone in the match agrees to it, and you're not playing in an official event, then there is really no harm. An important detail to remember: Make sure you establish whether or not you get "choosies," which means you get to play either one of the two balls you hit. Unless you do so, some players will insist you play the second ball—which might be worse than the first one.

Nassau: The most basic bet for match play, it has three points—the front nine, the back nine, and the total match—of equal dollar value up for grabs. The name, by the way, comes from Nassau Country Club in New York, where the betting game originated.

natural: A term usually reserved for describing a good score on a hole where you receive a handicap stroke(s). An example: You make a birdie three on a par four, and you get an additional shot off for your handicap, so you end up with a net two on the hole. You would say, "I made a natural three and got a shot, so I was net two for the hole."

net: This is your score for a hole after you deduct any handicap strokes. If you don't get any shots on a hole, your gross and net scores are the same.

one-point: Another way of describing a better-ball match.

one-up: If your match is tied going into the eighteenth hole and you win that hole, you won your match "one-up."

order of play: This is the order in which players take their turns playing their shots. In match play, it's important to adhere to it, because in certain situations it creates an advantage. The order of play never changes—the player who is farthest from the hole is always up.

pencil hockey: A player who lies about his score is said to be playing "pencil hockey."

pick it up: If you say this to someone, you're conceding his next shot.

pick up a pair: If you "pick up a pair," you won two points on a hole.

pigeon: For serious money players, a "pigeon" is someone they've identified as an easy mark, i.e., someone they're confident they can beat.

play 'em down: This means you'll play every ball as you find it, without improving the lie.

play it as it lies: It's the oldest Rule in golf, and it means just what it says. If someone in your group wants to play things differently, he should say so on the first tee. Otherwise, it's assumed that all in the group will play the ball as it lies.

play off the low ball: This means that everyone in the group determines the number of handicap strokes he will get by comparing his own handicap to that of the lowest handicap in the group. (See *handicap strokes.*)

point: A point refers to the number of betting units available, won, or lost on a given hole or in a given portion of a match. If you win a hole in a skins game, you win a point. If you win a hole with three carryovers, you win four points (the three plus the hole you won). If you win a hole in a Nassau, you haven't won any points. You win points when you win the front nine (one point), back nine (one point), and match (one point). A greenie or any other junk is also a point.

preferred lies: Another way of saying you're going to improve the lie of the ball, best declared before the start of a match.

press: A press begins a new match, worth one point, within the original match. The length of the press lasts as long as the part of the match for which the press is offered. In other words, if you're two down at the fourth tee and decide to press the front nine, that press bet ends after the ninth hole, just like the original bet.

ringer: Someone who is a much better match player than his handicap indicates. This is not to say he is cheating, but that some people have a knack for match play that cannot be fully described simply by using numbers. (The term *ringer,* by the way, goes all the way back to medieval times, when a king or a duke or a royal someone would enter an unknown expert archer into archery competitions. He would get his arrows into the center ring on the target, hence "ringer.")

roll 'em in the fairway *or* **roll 'em everywhere:** This means you can improve your lie either in the fairway only, or anywhere on the course, depending on which version you use. This should be agreed upon before the start of a match, and is only going to hurt you if you're the best player in the group.

sandbagger: A player who purposely posts falsely high scores in order to drive up his handicap. Basically, a cheater.

sandy: This describes the act of successfully getting up and down from a greenside bunker. Sometimes a sandy is worth a point of junk. (See *junk*.)

scats: A match-play game for three players, the scat is the point value of each hole. In other words, if you play one-dollar scats, each hole is worth one dollar. On any hole where there is a tie for low ball, the point is carried over.

setting them up: Yet another way of saying you'll be improving the lie of the ball.

side action *or* **side bets:** Any individual bets that are separate from the main team match are referred to as side bets or side action.

singles match: Just you versus another guy—no partner to bail you out.

skins: A game where individuals compete alone and fight for points or "skins" on each hole. Like scats, when two tie for the low ball, the point is carried over. The only difference between scats and skins is that in skins, the value of the points is increased over the course of the match. The usual order is to determine a point value for the first six holes, another point value for the second six holes (numbers seven through twelve), and a third point value for the final six holes. Typically, the amounts double or triple. An example: Skins on the first six holes are worth one dollar, skins on the second six holes are worth two or three dollars, and skins on the final six holes are worth five dollars.

MASTERS OF MATCH PLAY:
HALE IRWIN

With a Ryder Cup record of 13-5-2, Hale Irwin is one of the best players ever to compete in that event. (That's a .700 winning percentage.) The first time he ever played in the Ryder Cup, he won 4½ points (in 1975). Irwin also holds the unique niche of being the only player to win three U.S. Opens (1974, 1979, 1990). (Twelve players have won two Opens, and only four players, Willie Anderson, Bobby Jones, Ben Hogan, and Jack Nicklaus, have won four.) Irwin also won the old Piccadilly World Match Play event in 1974 and 1975.

Irwin is a tough-as-nails competitor. At the University of Colorado he was the 1967 NCAA golf champion *and* a two-time All Big-Eight selection as a defensive back on the school's football team! Clearly, Irwin is no run-of-the-mill Tour player, and has an attitude that is particularly suited to match play. They always say the defensive back is the loneliest position in football because he's on his own back there. Apparently, Irwin is comfortable relying on himself to win—four of his five losses in Ryder Cup play came when he had a partner. (In a weird aside, his only loss in singles play came at the hands of Brian Barnes, the same guy who beat Nicklaus twice in the same day.)

What you can learn from Hale Irwin

That Irwin won three U.S. Open titles signals one of the things that makes him a great player. The Open is played on long courses with firm greens, which means that players who can hit powerful, high long-iron approach shots have a great chance of winning. (Nicklaus is a fine example of this as well.) In 1974 at Winged Foot, with the tournament hanging in the balance, Irwin hit a two-iron to the final green and made his winning par with two putts. In 1990, at the sixteenth hole of his play-off with Mike Donald at Medinah, Irwin trailed by two shots. He needed a birdie in a bad way, and he rifled a two-iron approach to ten feet and made the putt for three. When Donald bogeyed the eighteenth, the two went to sudden death, which Irwin won with a birdie at the first hole. Two perfectly played long irons won those Opens for Irwin.

Many everyday players struggle with their long irons and fairway woods. In an interview with one of the coauthors of this book conducted for ABC Sports just after Irwin won the 1990 U.S. Open, Irwin talked about his superb long-iron play. His key pointers were as follows:

- Don't grip the club too tightly. When you do, you lose the feel of the clubhead, and it's important to feel the clubhead throughout the swing with the long irons. You want to feel as if you're making a "long" swing, and you can't do that if you can't feel the club.
- Position the ball forward in your swing, so you catch the ball slightly on the upswing. A good reference point is to play the ball off the inside of your left heel.
- The key during the swing is not to rush it. Take your time getting through the transition phase, when you shift from the backswing to the downswing. The ball isn't going anywhere until you hit it, so don't be in a hurry.
- Think of the takeaway and the swing into the ball as a "sweeping" action, as if you're going to sweep the club off the ground rather than stick it into the ground behind the ball.
- Make a full finish. Extend your arms through the ball and down the target line. Don't stop when you hit the ball—swing until you've completed your follow-through.

Another point that can help you is to open your stance slightly, aiming your body just to the left of your target. The ball will fade some, but this will make it easier for you to make a full finish, with your hands up high, next to your head.

sudden death: When a tournament match finishes the eighteenth hole all square, it proceeds to sudden death. In sudden death, the first player to win a hole is the winner of the match. If holes are halved, play continues until someone wins.

take it away: Another way of conceding a putt to your opponent.

thin to win: A saying that means, under pressure, you're better off hitting the ball thin than you are catching it fat. A thin shot still gets most of the carry and has some spin on it.

three-ball match: If you can't find a fourth player to round out your group, you can play a "three-ball," a match where you simultaneously compete at match play against the other two guys. This is not a two-tie all tie thing like skins, but rather two separate matches.

toss balls: A random method of determining partners for a match. Each player gives a ball to the player who is going to toss them in the air. He tosses them in the air and lets them hit the ground. The two balls that settle closest to each other are partners for that match.

two and one, three and two, four and three, etc.: This is the final score of a match. The first number is the number of holes by which the winner was ahead, and the second number is the number of holes that were remaining when the match was closed out. So, if you win a match four and three, you were four holes ahead with only three holes remaining. In match play, the match ends at that point. There's no point in continuing on to play the remaining holes.

Vegas: Perhaps the wildest gambling game of them all, it's fully described in the chapter on betting games. Bring your wallet and pick a good partner.

winter rules: In the off-season, a course may post a sign that reads "Play winter rules" or "Winter rules in effect." This means you can improve your lie "through the green," which means anywhere but in a hazard.

wolf: Another wild and fun betting game, fully described in the chapter on betting games. You don't have to be smart enough to pick a good partner for the entire match because you'll possibly have a different one on every hole.

GREAT MOMENTS IN THE RYDER CUP: 1993, AMERICA WINS IN ENGLAND FOR THE FIRST TIME SINCE 1981

For the U.S. Ryder Cup team, a visit to The Belfry, in Sutton Coldfield, England, had become comparable to a visit from the boogeyman—it was scary. In 1985 at The Belfry, the Europeans had thrashed the Americans 16½ to 11½, in the most embarrassing defeat the Americans ever suffered. In 1987, the European team did the unthinkable and won in the United States, at Muirfield Village. In 1989, the United States managed a tie at The Belfry (14–14), but that didn't mean much, since the Euros got to keep the Cup. In 1991, after Europe had held the Cup for eight years, the United States managed to win it back at Kiawah Island—but just barely. Bernhard Langer had to miss a six-foot putt on the last hole in order for them to do so. If Langer had made that putt, the matches would have been halved again. Which brings us to 1993 and The Belfry—Europe's happy hunting ground.

The captain in 1993 was Tom Watson, the man with the greatest British Open record in the modern era. Before the event, Watson declared he wanted players "with the hearts and guts" to play golf under pressure. The Americans opened the final round trailing 8½ to 7½, but they were confident entering a day that might be the best day of matches the Ryder Cup has ever seen. They were confident because after the second-day morning foursomes matches, the United States was down 7½ to 4½, and staring a blowout straight in the face. They rallied in the afternoon four-balls, with wins by Corey Pavin and Jim Gallagher, Jr., Raymond Floyd and Payne Stewart, and John Cook and Chip Beck. It was the win by Cook and Beck that got the Americans fired up, as it came against Nick Faldo and Colin Montgomerie, who up to that point had looked unbeatable. But Cook and Beck beat them two-up. That match, said Watson, "was the heart of our victory. We knew then we had the horse and the rider."

The singles matches were pure fireworks. Lanny Wadkins had to sit out because Sam Torrance of the European team had an infected toe. Their match was declared halved. Beck went out first and beat England's Barry Lane one-up, to draw the United States within a half point. Then it looked bad again for the Americans, as U.S. Open champ Lee Janzen lost to Montgomerie and Corey Pavin lost to twenty-five-year-old Peter Baker. Next, Freddie Couples halved Ian Woosnam, so the United States was still 2½ points down, and when Cook lost to Sweden's Joakim Haeegman, things weren't looking good at all for the United States. Then they caught fire—Stewart beat Mark James 3 and 2, and Davis Love III beat Constantino Rocca of Italy. And down the stretch they came.

Jim Gallagher, Jr., gave the Americans a shot of adrenaline with a 3 and 2 victory over Seve Ballesteros, the man at the heart of the European team. Then fifty-one-year-old Raymond Floyd, the oldest competitor in Ryder Cup history, ripped off three back-nine birdies to beat Jose Maria Olazabal, and both men of the Spanish Armada had been defeated. Tom Kite dusted Bernhard Langer 5 and 3, and the final match pitted gutsy Paul Azinger against Nick Faldo. Even though the matches had been decided when Azinger and Faldo were finishing up, "Zinger" wasn't about to lose. Faldo took the lead in their match with a hole-in-one at the fourteenth hole, but Azinger rallied to halve the match with a birdie at the final hole. And the Americans had done what they had failed to do in two previous trips to The Belfry: win.

Conclusion

The golf world is filled with people who obsess over shooting the lowest possible score for eighteen holes. It's easy to understand why. The biggest influence on the golfing masses is professional golf, the week-in and week-out object of which is to shoot the lowest score for a series of rounds. It's a lovely game for the Casper Milquetoasts of the world, but it lacks consistent drama because there is no direct confrontation between competitors. Strictly speaking, when played at stroke play the game leaves us wanting—it does not fulfill our most human desires.

Every person possesses some amount of competitive instinct. Match play offers a golfer the only true opportunity to exercise this quality within the context of his game. In stroke play, you compete against the course and, indirectly, the field. At the end of a stroke-play event the winner has gained a certain amount of satisfaction, but he doesn't get the emotional rush of having vanquished a foe. Certainly, winning the Masters or the U.S. Open is a thrilling thing for the winner, but the tens of millions of weekend golfers in the world will never have that experience. So how are they supposed to derive competitive satisfaction from the game? The answer is by winning at match play.

Match play allows you to compete against someone who fights back, not something that lays inanimate and waits for your mistakes. The golfer at match play is a warrior who takes the best blow his opponent can deal him, struggles to his feet, and returns fire. This exciting brand of golf provides you with an opportunity to be a hunter intelligently stalking his prey. It gives you a chance to use your wits, test your survival instincts, and challenge every element of your body/mind connection in an attempt to win. There is no need to kid yourself: Winning is what it's all about in match play. So the next time you hit the first tee, hitch up your boots and adapt the mind-set of

Sir Winston Churchill. Never give up. Never surrender. Never consider yourself out of the hole or out of the match. Use the information in this book to turn every fiber of your soul toward becoming the ultimate golf warrior. Commit yourself to winning every time you play, and you will never again view the game the same way.

Index